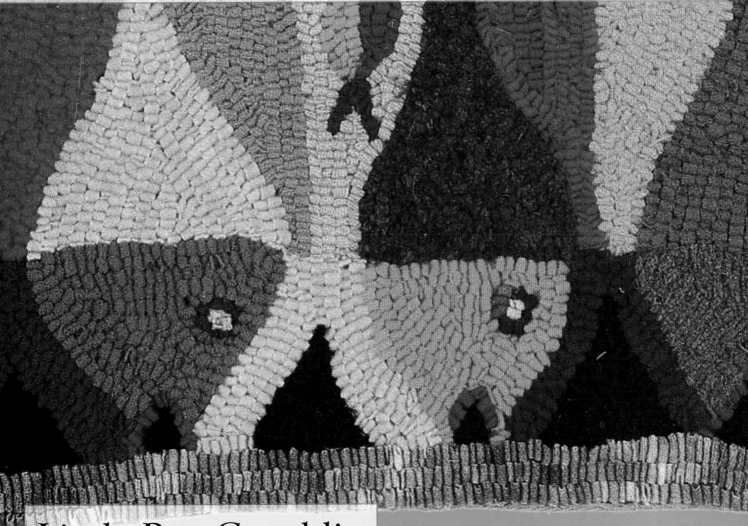

Contemporary Hooked Rugs

Themes and Memories

Linda Rae Coughlin

Schiffer Publishing Ltd

4880 Lower Valley Road, Atglen, PA 19310 USA

Dedication

To Patty Yoder
May 30, 1943 – March 20, 2005

"Your presence in the rug hooking world raised the bar so
many levels. We all thank you."

Other Schiffer Books on Related Subjects
Hooked on Rugs: Outstanding Contemporary Designs, by Jessie A. Turbayne
The Big Book of Hooked Rugs: 1950-1980s, by Jessie A. Turbayne
The Complete Guide to Collecting Hooked Rugs: Unrolling the Secrets, by Jessie A. Turbayne
The Hooker's Art: Evolving Designs in Hooked Rugs, by Jessie A. Turbayne
Hooked Rug Treasury, by Jessie A. Turbayne
Hooked Rugs: History and the Continuing Tradition, by Jessie A. Turbayne
Hooked Rugs Today, by Amy Oxford
Punch Needle Rug Hooking: Techniques and Designs, by Amy Oxford

Front cover artists: (top) Charlene Marsh; (middle row, left to right) Patty Yoder,
Kazuko Kaneko, Assadulla Nekaien; (bottom row, left to right) Patty Yoder, Deanne
Fitzpatrick.

Back cover artists: (top) Louisa Creed, Gail Dufresne; (bottom) Sarah Province.

Title page artist: Debra Marrone

Copyright © 2007 by Linda Rae Coughlin
Library of Congress Control Number: 2006929600

Designed by Mark David Bowyer
Type set in Van Dijk / Arrus BT

ISBN: 0-7643-2557-4
Printed in China

Published by Schiffer Publishing Ltd.
4880 Lower Valley Road
Atglen, PA 19310
Phone: (610) 593-1777; Fax: (610) 593-2002
E-mail: Info@schifferbooks.com

For the largest selection of fine reference books on this
and related subjects, please visit our web site at **www.
schifferbooks.com**
We are always looking for people to write books on
new and related subjects. If you have an idea for a book
please contact us at the above address.

This book may be purchased from the publisher.
Include $3.95 for shipping.
Please try your bookstore first.
You may write for a free catalog.

In Europe, Schiffer books are distributed by
Bushwood Books
6 Marksbury Ave.
Kew Gardens
Surrey TW9 4JF England
Phone: 44 (0) 20 8392-8585; Fax: 44 (0) 20 8392-
9876

Contents

Acknowledgments

I would like to thank the following people for all their help in making this book possible. Carol Glennon, for designing a program to help me keep track of all the images and text for this book. I am also grateful to Carol for her other expert skills, which have been an invaluable part of getting this book completed. Jessie Turbayne, for opening the door for me to Schiffer Publishing and for all the support, encouragement, and knowledge she has shared with me over the years. Ramsey Yoder, for being so generous and working tirelessly to get me all the slides and details needed to showcase Patty Yoder's talent. Donna Baker, my editor, for her help creating this book.

Kind acknowledgments to all artists, curators, photographers, and others who are a part of this book and have been so helpful with getting me all that was needed to make this book possible: Georgie Abbiati, Jill Aiken, Mary Raymond Alenstein, Ricketta Algarva, Cosette Allen, Susan Andreson, Hiroshi Ariyoshi, Nancy Bachand, Jean Barber, Rita Barnard, Carole K. Bartolovich, Norma Batastini, Donna Lee Beaudoin, Patsy Becker, Barbara Benner, Elizabeth Black, Anne Boissinot, Barbara Boll-Ingber, Kathy Boozan, Pierrette Bortolussi, Marilyn Bottjer, Betty Bouchard, Jeanne Bourgeois, Shirley Bradshaw, Regina Broussard, Judi Brownell, Loretta Bucceri, Diane Burgess, Nicole Butler, Cilla Cameron, Susan Carson, Pamela Carter, Claudia Casebolt, Burma Cassidy, Cecille Caswell, Shirley Chaiken, Lucy Clark, Cecilia Evan Clement, Willadine Cochran, Cecely Conrad, Amy Stoner Cotter, Martha Crawford, Louisa Creed, Gloria E. Crouse;

Dorothy Danforth, Barbara D'Arcy, Davey De-Graff, Eugenie Delaney, Marilyn Denning, Margaret Dickerson, Kazuko DiCroce, Happy DiFranza, Steve DiFranza, Tom di Maria, Suzanne Dirmaier, Lory Doolittle, Anne Douglas, Lyle Drier, Kim Dubay, Gail Dufresne, Doris Eaton, Elizabeth Edwards, Ruth Emerson, Ann Erskine, Erma C. Estwick, Jeanne Fallier, Qing Fan-Dollinger, Carol Feeney, Susan Feller, Gail Ferdinando, Jeanne Field, Patti Ann Finch, Deanne Fitzpatrick, Joan Frankenthal, Ruth Frost, Kumiko Fujita, Mitsue Fukuda, Setsuko Fukuda, Miharu Fuwa;

Florine Gagnon, Robin Garcia, Paul Gee, Karl Gimber, Mary Jo Gimber, Susan Gingras, Line Godbout, Jorge Gomez, Gloria Gonzalez, Jan Graham, Éveline Haché-Lachance, Fumiyo Hachisuka, Ann Hallett, Jane Halliwell, Daniel Hamilton, Nancy A. Harland, Cindy Harpring, Rae Reynolds Harrell, Carol Harvey-Clark, Joan Hebert, Nola Heidbreder, Priscilla Heininger, Nancy L. Himmelsbach, Fuka Hiraoka, Camille Holvoet, Gail H. Horton, Grace Hostetter, Mary Hulette, Peg Irish;

Carrie Bell Jacobus, Tracy Jamar, E. Germaine James, Sue Janssen, Cedric Johnson, Kazuko Kaneko, Joyce Kapadia, Takiko Kawama, Eriko Keino, Deborah Kelley, Diane S. Kelly, Margaret Kenny, Wanda Kerr, Shizuko Kimura, Mary Klotz, Kazuko Kobayashi, Kei Kobayashi, Jackie Kojis, Sally Kraimer, Stephanie Ashworth Krauss, Lonny Krogman, Joyce Krueger, Cyndi Melendy Labelle, Gail Duclos Lapierre, Sharon Laufer, Sue Lawler, Thérèsa Arsenault Léger, Rosemary Levin, Maryanne Lincoln, Sandy Lincoln, Joan Lindsay, Laurie Ling, Anne-Marie W. Littenberg, Roslyn Logsdon, Mary Logue, Margaret Lutz;

Sylvia M. Macdonald, Helen Mach, Susan Mackey, Dwight Mackintosh, Susan Marks, Debra Marrone, Charlene Marsh, John Martin, Karen T. Martin, Harumi Matsui, Maria Matzkin, Mollie "Lee" McBride, Lea H. McCrone, Maggie McLea, Sybil Mercer, Pat Merikallio, Michele Micarelli, Jo-Ann Millen, Lisa Mims, Polly Minick, Donald Mitchell, Tomoka Miyamoto, Noriko Mizuno, Joan Mohrmann, Elizabeth Morgan, Angela Mork, Carol M. Munson, Yvonne Muntwyler, Haruyo Murata, Hiromi Murata, June Myles, Madaka Nagumo, Assadulla Nekaien, Kim Nixon, Doris Norman, Betty Oberstar, Kathleen O'Brien, Francine Oken, Celia Oliver, Nancy Oppedisano, Danielle Ouellet, Amy Oxford;

Joanna Palmer, Gail Papetti, Dolores Park, Mary Parker, Deanie Pass, Donald Paterson, Père-Edgar-T.-Leblanc School, Diane Phillips, Linda Pietz, Marielle R. Poirier, Barbara D. Pond, Kay F. Porter, Sarah Province, Mary Querques, Karen Quigley, Carmen Quinones, Judy Quintman, Nancy Reding, Denise Reithofer, Linda Repasky, Phyllis Riley, Heather

Ritchie, Emily K. Robertson, Michael Robertson, Sandra Robinson, Julie Rogers, Hazel Rooker, Olga Rothschild, Miriam "Dolly" Rowe, Alice Rudell, Ann Rudolph;

Hiromi Sakamoto, Eric H. Sandberg, Taeko Sano, Andrea Sargent, Mary Sargent, Hiroko Sato, Nobuko Sato, Évangéline Savoie, Arlene Scanlon, Linda Friedman Schmidt, Robin Schwamb, Iris Simpson, Diane R. Skalak, Susan L. Smidt, Jule Marie Smith, Roberta Smith, Marian Specter, Cindy Spence, Gerone Spruill, St. Thérèsa School, Peggy Stanilonis, Joan Stocker, Theresa Strack, Laurie M. Sybertz, Marie "Allene" Thibeault, Cecelia K. Toth, Sharon L. Townsend, Sachiko Toyoda, Nelson Tygart, William Tyler;

Abby Vakay, Ronald Veasey, Mary Ellen Von Holt, Kay Wachowiak, Bernice Wallman, Suzanne Wallner, Debbie Walsh, Grace Ward, JoAnne Watson, Joan Wheeler, Johanna White, Margo White, Alexandra Whitelock, Shirley Wiedemann, Elizabeth E. Williams, Elizabeth Williamson, George Wilson, Ann Winterling, Rose Wirtz, Ed Wissner, Helen Wolfel, Elizabeth Wrathall, Mutsumi Yamamoto, Maureen Yates, Patty Yoder, Shirley H. Zandy, Roya Zarrehparvar, Nancy Zickler, Suzanne Ziegler.

A special thanks to Burma Cassidy, Susan Feller, Carrie Jacobus, Emily Robertson, and Rose Wirtz, for their creative input and friendship. They were very patient and always had the time to listen to me when I needed to bounce ideas off them. Thank you to my dear grandmother, Alice, who first introduced me to fiber when I was a young child and continued to share in its joys with me over the years. And finally, a very special thank you to my patient and loving husband, Jerry Coughlin, who has always encouraged me in my art and has been there for me every step of the way.

Introduction

This book showcases a wonderful selection of the contemporary, theme-related collections and series rugs that have been created in the past few years. One might ask, "How were the rugs selected to be part of this book?" *Webster's Dictionary* defines a collection as, "an accumulation of objects gathered for study, comparison or exhibition." Webster then goes on to define a series as, "a number of things of the same class coming one after another in succession." This book includes rugs in both of these broad categories.

Many of the rugs were created by groups of artists who joined together to complete a theme-related project in a defined amount of time, usually with a few set parameters like color, size, finishing techniques, and subject matter. Also included are fiber artists who have worked on their own to explore a theme-related subject, using self-imposed parameters that only they needed to follow. Such individual theme-related series tend to be part of an ongoing series—typically, the artist has been creating pieces for some time using the same subject matter and finds that she or he has an unlimited amount of ideas to explore within these limitations. On the other hand, the group series tend to include everyone from the seasoned artist to the person who might have just learned how to hook.

These collections provide a fascinating look at how one subject can be explored in so many different ways. They also become important educational tools with respect to style, technique, and subject matter. Some have specific stories to tell, but on the whole, most of the rug collections featured in this book are intended to be viewed solely for visual enjoyment. In parts of the book I have added detailed text, most times in the artist's own words, but in many cases the visual impact of the work speaks for itself. Also featured are examples of rugs that are not part of a collection or series, but do relate to similar themes and are important because of their unique designs and subject matter.

This extraordinary art form brings joy to all who are touched by it, from serious artists using it as a creative outlet to novices just picking up a rug hook for the first time. Artists, children, students, the able-bodied and the disabled—all with varying degrees of talent—can experience firsthand this exciting medium. People create for all types of reasons and with many different intentions. Hence, some of the collections in this book are playful in nature, others are serious, and still others have been created to preserve and document a moment in time. Despite their individuality, one thing they have in common is their rich, exciting appeal to all who delight in superbly crafted hooked rugs.

Creating this book has been an extension of my ongoing desire to have rug hooking recognized as an art form. I am very grateful for the opportunity to showcase some of the wonderful collections that currently exist. I can remember the first time I attended a hooked rug show some fifteen years ago, and all the joys and frustrations I went through trying to find the needed materials, tools, and even a teacher to get started. I am thrilled that today there are so many books, schools, workshops, and even the Internet to help the newly interested get started. The process of making rugs has also changed—what used to be the construction of practical items primarily used in the home has developed into a new and stimulating art form being showcased in galleries and museums. Yet with all this newfound recognition, rug hooking still retains its original function as a way to create beautiful coverings for the floor.

Some of the collections featured here have never been viewed by the public or have had only limited exposure; others have been exhibited both nationally and internationally. It is my hope that the rugs in this book will speak for themselves and that you will find joy in viewing them. It is with great pleasure that I have been given the opportunity to bring these collections together for all to enjoy and appreciate.

—Linda Rae Coughlin

Please note that sizes of the rugs have been rounded to the nearest inch, with the height of the rug preceding width, unless otherwise noted. Collections in this book are not necessarily complete.

Chapter One

The ABC's

The Alphabet of Sheep by Patty Yoder

Patty Yoder crafted some thirty-five rugs between 1992 and March 2005. This series of twenty-six pieces was originally created for a children's book that Patty self-published in 2003, called *The Alphabet of Sheep*. Using Patty's favorite subject matters—family, friends, and her beloved animals—this extraordinary series took nine years to complete. It's an amazing body of work, clearly showing Patty's wonderful eye for color and design and her true mastery of the techniques of rug hooking. Beyond that, Patty was a friend to many in the rug hooking world. With the passing of Patty Yoder, her husband Ramsey has generously allowed this wonderful collection to be showcased here.

Photography courtesy of Ramsey Yoder.

> *Numbers in each caption refer to the order in which each piece in this series was created.*

A is for Anthony, As in Susan B. 50" x 23". By Patty Yoder, Tinmouth, Vermont. #19 in the series. The Statue of Liberty, as a single ewe with a young lamb at her side.

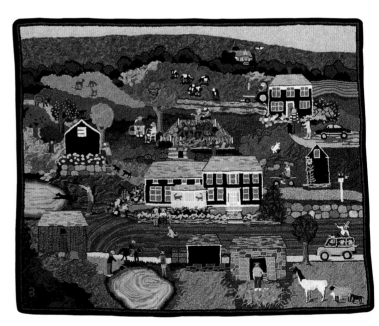

B is for Brad and Brett. 39" x 48". By Patty Yoder, Tinmouth, Vermont. #13 in the series. The Yoder's family, friends, and animals on their farm in Vermont.

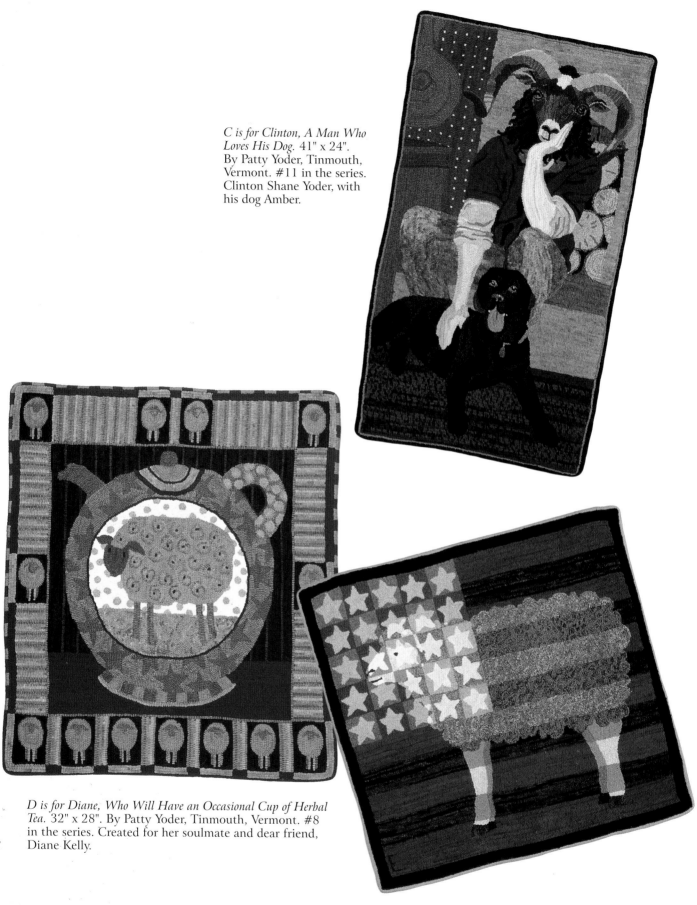

C is for Clinton, A Man Who Loves His Dog. 41" x 24". By Patty Yoder, Tinmouth, Vermont. #11 in the series. Clinton Shane Yoder, with his dog Amber.

D is for Diane, Who Will Have an Occasional Cup of Herbal Tea. 32" x 28". By Patty Yoder, Tinmouth, Vermont. #8 in the series. Created for her soulmate and dear friend, Diane Kelly.

E is for Ernie, A Patriotic Young Ram Who Only Has Eyes for Bonnie. 30" x 33". By Patty Yoder, Tinmouth, Vermont. #18 in the series. Ernie and Bonnie, the Yoder's best friends, who bring everyone they meet great joy and understanding.

8

F is for Frank and His Friends in the Upper Barn. 37" x 46". By Patty Yoder, Tinmouth, Vermont. #24 in the series. This rug represents the eight animals that live in the Yoder's upper barn.

H is for Hannah and Sarah, A Civil Union. 32" x 32". By Patty Yoder, Tinmouth, Vermont. #23 in the series. Created for the state of Vermont, with hope for the future of the United States of America.

G is for Glady, Always a Blue Ribbon Ewe. 48" x 27". By Patty Yoder, Tinmouth, Vermont. #16 in the series. Named after Patty's mother, who was a great strength in her life.

I is for Ian, Who Had a Great Time on His Way to Tipperary. 30" x 44". By Patty Yoder, Tinmouth, Vermont. #25 in the series. Ian is a make-believe ram inspired by an Irish fellow, the Yoder's driver during a trip to Ireland.

> *In this piece, Patty shows true mastery and control in the use of color.*

J is for Joseph, Who Is a Coat of Many Colors. 30" x 33". By Patty Yoder, Tinmouth, Vermont. #9 in the series. Inspired by a memorable dyeing lesson with friend Maryanne Lincoln, where they created a gorgeous rainbow of colors of dyed wool.

K is for Kristin, Who Enjoys Some Time Alone. 27" x 22". By Patty Yoder, Tinmouth, Vermont. #26 in the series. This rug is for one of the most "together" women Patty knows: Kristin, a seventh and eighth grade science teacher who is loved and appreciated by her students.

L is for Lydia. 43" x 31". By Patty Yoder, Tinmouth, Vermont. #2 in the series. Inspired by the many sheep of New Zealand, this elegant beast was named after Patty's great aunt Lydia, a tall and beautiful woman with "a chiseled face and huge ears."

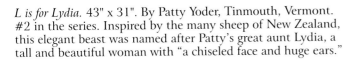

M is for Moonlight, A Woman of Unusual Self-Esteem. 26" x 27". By Patty Yoder, Tinmouth, Vermont. #1 in the series. Moonlight, the first member of the Yoder's family of sheep.

N is for Nichols. 22" x 28". By Patty Yoder, Tinmouth, Vermont. #17 in the series. Inspired by a dear friend, Junior Nichols, a retired dairy farmer in the town of Dorset, Vermont.

O is for Ogden. 35" x 29". By Patty Yoder, Tinmouth, Vermont. #4 in the series. Inspired by Ogden Nash's poem, "Little Gambling Lamb."

P is for Polly. 23" x 32". By Patty Yoder, Tinmouth, Vermont.
#5 in the series. This piece was created for Patty's friend Polly
Minick, to honor her primitive style of hooking.

R is for Ramsey, A Gentle Shepherd. 50" x 35". By Patty
Yoder, Tinmouth, Vermont. #6 in the series. Ramsey
Yoder and Toby in front of their old upper barn,
which burned to the ground during their first year
of lambing.

Q is for Quinella. 25" x 20". By Patty Yoder, Tinmouth, Vermont.
#15 in the series. "This is a happy rug."

U is for Ursula, Always the Underdog. 15" x 18". By Patty Yoder, Tinmouth, Vermont. #21 in the series. Ursula and the Yoder's little white dog, Jesse, under the big top.

S is for Sandy, Santa's Favorite. 44" x 29". By Patty Yoder, Tinmouth, Vermont. #3 in the series. Santa carrying a bag of new baby lambs to put in Christmas stockings.

T is for Toby. 31" x 50". By Patty Yoder, Tinmouth, Vermont. #7 in the series. A self-portrait of Patty with Toby, a black Suffolk ram and her four legged friend.

V is for Victor, A Natural Vegetarian. 39" x 51". By Patty Yoder, Tinmouth, Vermont. #10 in the series. Inspired by the painting, *The Summer,* by Giuseppe Arcimbaldo.

X is for Xanadu, A Remarkable Ram. 51" x 42". By Patty Yoder, Tinmouth, Vermont. #22 in the series. Charlotte, from *Charlotte's Web,* was the inspiration for this rug.

W is for Wally, A Flying Horticulturalist. 36" x 34". By Patty Yoder, Tinmouth, Vermont. #14 in the series. Inspired by a rare day in the late summer of 1997, when thousands of butterflies stopped at the Yoder's farm during their fall migration.

Y is for Yoder, Lydia's Family Name. 40" x 37". By Patty Yoder, Tinmouth, Vermont. #20 in the series. This piece was inspired by Chuck Close's early portrait work.

> *Patty preferred to use flat-colored wool in her rugs and very rarely used mottled wool.*

Z is for Zonie. 33" x 42". By Patty Yoder, Tinmouth, Vermont. #12 in the series. Created to give the feel of a cover from *The New Yorker* magazine.

Other ABC Rugs

These two rugs are examples of pieces from a series of forty-two mats curated by JoAnne Watson. They were created to depict the ABC's of different countries around the world.

Belize. 12" x 12". By Gail Dufresne, Lambertville, New Jersey. 2002. *Photography by Linda Rae Coughlin.*

Australia. 12" x 12". By Tracy Jamar, New York City, New York. 2003. Australia is often described as having a red center with a fringe of green around it. The boundaries of the states are delineated by using wool, yarn, t-shirts, novelty fabric, and beads at the capitals. *Courtesy of Tracy Jamar.*

Chapter Two

Our Four-Legged Friends

Animals are so important to many of us and are a common theme when it comes to creating rugs.

The Story of Lucky by Rosemary Levin

Entirely self-taught, Rosemary Levin creates hooked rugs that are unique. Her art is untouched by any influences outside of herself and her environment. All of her designs tend to use bright clean colors and pure graphic lines. Rosemary has completed more than one hundred rugs in the past six years and the "Lucky" series is a wonderful expression of her passion.

Of this series, Rosemary writes:

For my fortieth birthday, my husband, Garry, gave me a black and white dog piñata, with a tag reading "IOU" around its neck. This was Garry's way of saying it was time for us to have a family dog. We looked in the local pet stores and at the Humane Society, and we answered ads for a year, but were unable to find our dog.

Around this time I received word that my father was terminally ill. Although it had been many years since we had talked, I decided to call him. After getting through the difficulties of reconnection, I began telling him about our search for a dog. He told me he had been breeding Border Collies for the past few years and had a puppy he thought would be perfect for us. The next morning Lucky was on a plane from Dothan, Alabama, arriving in Bangor, Maine, just before midnight. When Lucky came off the plane, she was standing in her kennel looking out at us with the most soulful eyes I had ever seen. I wondered if she had been standing with anticipation for the entire flight.

Lucky rode home with us and embarked on her new life. Since she had grown up on a farm, she was not used to being allowed in the house, much less up on the furniture. And although she had been around horses, cows, and other dogs, she had never shared space with two cats. However, Lucky was very gentle and adjusted immediately to her new family and life in Maine. Each morning and afternoon, she walked our daughter to and from school. She chased squirrels, herded waves on the beach, walked with me to the art gallery where I worked, and became known throughout town. She loved to hike the trails of Downeast Maine with us, and when we got kayaks, she would ride in mine as we paddled about, wearing her bright red life vest and drawing applause from everyone who saw us. She went with us to Elmira, New York, for our daughter's first day of college, to four years of parents' weekends, and to graduation. She became such a part of our lives, it is a wonder how we ever lived without her.

In the fall of 2003, Lucky became the central inspiration for my art. She is extremely expressive and loves to pose for me as I sketch her. These sketches became the Lucky rugs series. Each piece is made with hand-dyed wool and includes bits of Lucky's fur and my hair, which a friend has spun into yarn.

Thinking back, my "Lucky" rugs were filled with many unintended coincidences. The seven rugs were started seven years after my father passed away. I hooked the first six during a seven month period this past winter, and started the last rug of the series in the early spring after many distractions and repeatedly redesigning this rug. After a scare with Lucky's health, she is now healthy and I have incorporated my cache of Lucky's tags into this last rug.

Lucky continues to enrich our lives. She keeps us healthy and fit. She comforts us and brings us pleasure and entertainment. She is our constant companion, and has become a friend to the many wonderful people who make up our Maine community.

Photography and artist statement courtesy of Rosemary Levin.

Golden Clouds. 24" x 24". By Rosemary Levin, Corea, Maine. 2004. "Sometimes the sun can make the clouds look golden. Lucky in the kayak with her bright red life vest is always ready to lead the way."

Snow Shadows. 24" x 24". By Rosemary Levin, Corea, Maine. 2005. "I saw Lucky running in the woods after a great snowfall. The shadows on the snow made by the trees inspired this rug."

Red Car. 24" x 24". By Rosemary Levin, Corea, Maine. 2004. "If Lucky had a car, I am sure it would be red and it would go fast."

Red Pumpkins. 24" x 24". By Rosemary Levin, Corea, Maine. 2004. "My friend Marion grew and gave me a huge red pumpkin. My friend Linda Rae taught me how to dye wool and gave me the teal wool. This rug honors friendship."

Scarlet Fields. 24" x 24". By Rosemary Levin, Corea, Maine. 2005. "Fall in Maine, the blueberry barrens (fields) turn scarlet. It is our favorite time of the year for long afternoon walks."

Purple and Gold Lucky #7. 22" x 48". By Rosemary Levin, Corea, Maine. 2005. "Purple and gold are important colors in our lives; our daughter's college colors and Lucky's dog tags. The 'IOU' tag was added as a symbolic element. Seven years we have loved Lucky, seven years since my father's death, seven rugs."

Green Fields and Indigo Skies. 24" x 24". By Rosemary Levin, Corea, Maine. 2004. "After attending an indigo dye workshop, I did this first 'Lucky' rug."

> *Know that you will have times when you're not feeling too creative. Take this ride; enjoy this time of being quiet. This is an important part of the creative process.*

The DiFranzas' Cat Series

Five rugs designed by Steve DiFranza and hooked
by Happy DiFranza with a cat theme.
Photography courtesy of The DiFranzas.

Morris Cat. 18" x 34". By Happy DiFranza, North Reading, Massachusetts. 2004. This piece shows a very sophisticated black cat sitting against a background inspired by William Morris.

The Boys. 18" x 34". By Happy DiFranza, North Reading, Massachusetts. 2003. These gentlemen have gathered in a landscape.

The Girls. 18" x 34". By Happy DiFranza, North Reading, Massachusetts. 2005. These three ladies sit before a quilt-like background.

The Oriental Rug Cats. 18" x 34". By Happy DiFranza, North Reading, Massachusetts. 2002. These two cats lounge against a quasi-oriental background.

Cat Family. 18" x 34". By Happy DiFranza, North Reading, Massachusetts. 2001. This family of felines has gathered in the lovely garden.

Rosie & Her Ancestors by Louisa Creed

"Rosie and Her Ancestors" came about after Louisa had a visit with her brother, Tim Nicholson. Tim, noticing the large quantity of cat rugs that Louisa had created, decided to photograph some of them and play with the images on his computer. He then came up with the idea of a "family tree" for Rosie, Louisa's cat, who had died some twelve years before. Rosie is featured with her imaginary relatives and is the inspiration for this rag rug series.

Having started with her first old cat, Rosie, Louisa has created some thirty-two pieces in this series, some of which are shown here. Working with primarily recycled wool, Louisa started creating her cats in 1989 and to date has hooked over one hundred of these four-legged friends into rugs.

Photography courtesy of Louisa Creed.

Rosie Appleby. 45" x 35". By Louisa Creed, York, England. 1989. The first cat in this series.

Mabel Mouser. 36" x 51". By Louisa Creed, York, England. 1990.

Lionel Illingworth. 39" x 53". By Louisa Creed,
York, England. 1992.

Julia Illingworth. 42" x 52". By Louisa Creed,
York, England. 1997.

Murphy Eaton. 53" x 39". By Louisa Creed,
York, England. 1995.

Tom Illingworth. 39" x 54". By Louisa Creed, York, England. 1998.

Twelve Cats. 47" x 58". By Louisa Creed, York, England. 1998.

George Appleby. 30" x 24". By Louisa Creed, York, England. 1999.

Harriet Creep. 31" x 26". By Louisa Creed, York, England. 1999.

William Appleby. 33" x 31". By Louisa Creed, York, England. 2000.

Horace Kitson. 32" x 24". By Louisa Creed, York, England. 2000.

Spencer Eaton. 20" x 20". By Louisa Creed, York, England.

Molly Mouser. 20" x 20". By Louisa Creed, York, England. 2000.

Wendy Kitson. 20" x 20". By Louisa Creed, York, England. 2000.

Jeremy Creep. 20" x 20". By Louisa Creed, York, England. 2000.

Owen Mouser. 20" x 20". By Louisa Creed, York, England. 2000.

Theresa Patterson. 20" x 20". By Louisa Creed, York, England. 2000.

Solomon Appleby. 20" x 20". By Louisa Creed, York, England. 2000.

Mary Oliver. 20" x 20". By Louisa Creed, York, England. 2000.

Chapter Three

Creative Growth Art Center

Shown in this chapter are examples of true folk art. Many of the pieces are narrative and have a story to tell, often in the artist's own words. These artists are creating their art, showing their art, and selling their art. They are to be applauded. While many people talk about creating some day, these artists serve as examples for all who wish to create but, for whatever reason, have never started.

The Art of the Creative Growth Art Center

Tom di Maria, Executive Director of Creative Growth Art Center, describes this organization and its unique rug hooking program as follows:

Creative Growth Art Center in Oakland, California serves more than 140 adult artists with developmental and psychiatric disabilities, and is the first independent art studio of its kind in the world. Since 1974, the studio program has offered painting, sculpture, ceramics, woodwork, video, and other creative opportunities to our community in a 10,000 square foot industrial work studio and gallery. Creative Growth's rug program was started in 1982 by visiting artist George Sommers as a way to further engage our artists in a broad spectrum of art making activities.

Creative Growth's rug program is unique within the program as it offers a collaborative team approach to design and production. Original artwork by any Creative Growth artist may be selected to serve as the design of a rug. Once chosen, the original artwork serves as a model and the rug artist crafts a rug based on the original design.

The making of the rug is accomplished in teams, with more than one maker working on each rug surface. Under the guidance of staff member Tara Tucker, the rugs are interpreted to transmit the spirit of the original art while offering qualities intrinsic to the feel, touch, and look of the newly created fiber artwork. All the rugs were created with wool and acrylic yarn and were hooked into a monk's cloth foundation

Over the years, the program has garnered increasing success and recognition. The artists' rugs are now in the collections of The White House, Prince Andrew of England, and Johns Hopkins Hospital, and have been featured in *O At Home* magazine, *Paper* magazine and Moss Gallery in New York. New designs are developed continually and commissions for specific designs are welcome.

Photography courtesy of Creative Growth Art Center.

Chicken Feed #1. 30" x 41". By Ricketta Algarva, Oakland, Califorina. 2003. "Ricketta Algarva kept some chickens many years ago. Her life history becomes part of the subject matter in her artwork. Ricketta is an active square dancer. She lives with her sister and a cat named Omelet."

Fish Story #1. 33" x 42". By Paul Gee, Oakland, California. 2005. "Paul Gee is known for his colorful fish with big teeth, and for the love of his mother. While at Creative Growth he was interested mostly in ceramics and assisting with maintenance of the ceramics studio."

Spring Showers. 44" x 33". By Regina Broussard, Oakland, California. 1993. "A pack-rat by nature, Regina Broussard has a fascination with food and squirrels. Both motifs reoccur regularly throughout her body of work. It is possible that the collecting nature of a squirrel speaks to Regina's own habitual collecting and has become a self identifying symbol within her art."

Manos Juntos #2. 39" x 30". By Jorge Gomez, Oakland, California. 1993. "Cuban born, Jorge Gomez creates a world of imaginary people smoking Cuban cigars and outfitted in whimsical clothes. Jorge is a romantic and his rug designs are often chosen for their strong relationship content and graphic quality."

Twins #1. 31" x 38". By Daniel Hamilton, Oakland, California. 2003. "Daniel Hamilton works mostly with ceramics at the Creative Growth Art Center. His strikingly beautiful human and animal forms have become vividly memorable rugs. Daniel is originally from Argentina and often visits there with his mother."

Reina De Angeles #1. 45" x 38". By Gloria Gonzalez, Oakland, California. 1993. "Gloria is a young and very talented artist at Creative Growth. She is a member of the rug department and has been creating and producing many intricate and challenging rug designs herself."

Gator in a Tub #1. 32" x 46". By Camille Holvoet, Oakland, California. 1989. "All of Camille's work is narrative. She takes what she sees in her own life and translates it into a fantastical world where alligators live in bathtubs."

Abstract #1. 53" x 41". By Cedric Johnson, Oakland, California. 2005. "Cedric Johnson often makes large colorful abstract drawings in Prismacolors. He also uses a similar semi-abstract style to draw portraits of imaginary people. Cedric is a large and colorful character in the studio. His voice is distinctive and he loves to carry on a good conversation."

Green Angel. 31" x 17". By Dwight Mackintosh, Oakland, California. 1988. "A legend at Creative Growth, Dwight Mackintosh lived in a world of line drawn people and his own written language. He made so many drawings that they littered the floor around him."

A predictable design can become boring to both the artist and the viewer. When our art takes some risks, it tells us more about who we are as a person.

Great White #6. 27" x 54". By John Martin, Oakland, California. 2004. "John Martin is a prolific artist at Creative Growth. His mostly narrative subject matter often combines organic forms with inorganic machines and tools. These hybrid animals, people, and tool forms become new characters that offer a glimpse into John's family, desires, and obsessions."

Untitled #1. 33" x 43". By Donald Mitchell, Oakland, California. 1996. "Donald often doesn't say anything while working in the studio, but hides his talent for singing the blues like he hides the stories behind his cluster of simplified people. You can ask him what it's all about, but most often he will just smile. Donald absorbs ideas and images from his surroundings and from found photographs, then uses pen and paper to express what he sees."

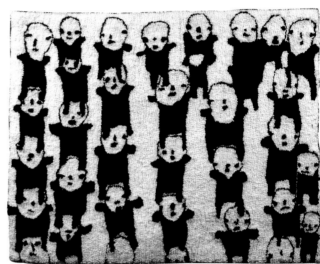

Eve #1. 39" x 31". By Assadulla Nekaien, Oakland, California. 1990. "Originally from Afghanistan, Assadulla Nekaien uses a strong sense of history and culture in the intricate details of his work. Nekaien's rug designs are both challenging and among the most beautiful."

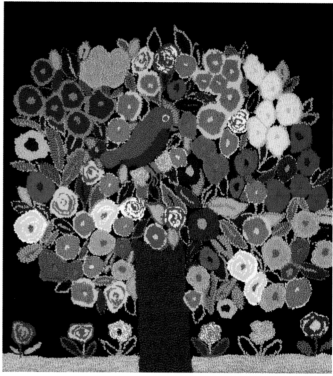

Beautiful Spring #3. 41" x 40". By Carmen Quinones, Oakland, California. 1995. "Carmen Quinones embraces her Mexican-American heritage and culture. She creates elaborate drawings and paintings of colorful flowers and religious imagery. Carmen is often thought of as the token 'Grandmother' of the Creative Growth Art Center studio. She knows everyone's name and personal history."

Dream Flowers #3. 42" x 30". By Kathleen O'Brien, Oakland, California. 1993. "Kathleen O'Brien always greets her friends with a 'Hello Honey.' Kathleen incorporates imagery of children, flowers, and animals into colorful vignettes. She has been a rug department member for many years."

Adam's Apple #2. 36" x 45". By Donald Paterson, Oakland, California. 1991. "Donald Paterson was for many years one of Creative Growth's most prolific rug designers. The graphic quality of his paintings lent themselves well to rug making. During his long career at Creative Growth, Donald was also one of the original Rug Project artisans, learning the rug making skills from George Sommers, the visiting artist that started the Creative Growth rug program."

Brut Love #1. 34" x 42". By Gerone Spruill, Oakland, California. 2004. "An Oakland, California native, Gerone's history of city life spills into his comic-like world of 'Chocolate City.' A gang of Gerone's well-drawn characters go through life in Chocolate City pursuing ideas about love, foot worship and 1970s disco music."

Let go! Suspend judgment.

Tom Cat #1. 33" x 41". By Nelson Tygart, Oakland, California. 2005. "Nelson was a young man with a big presence at Creative Growth. His painted wood cutouts, ceramic sculpture, and nearly abstract drawings and paintings of animals with their bold color and graphic quality have become some of the most quintessential 'Outsider' designs of the Creative Growth rug department."

The Imposter Chicken is Running Away From the Law With the Egg #1. 34" x 41". By William Tyler, Oakland, California. 2000. "William Tyler and his twin, Richard, are both artists at Creative Growth. William uses Richard and himself as recurring subjects in his fantastical artwork. William also has imposter chickens, camp, magic, and maps in his often series-oriented work."

Sheep #!. 30" x 49". By Ronald Veasey, Oakland, California. 2005. "Ronald Veasey is a proficient drawer of animals. He has a sensitive use of line that lends itself well to rug making. Ron is a quiet unassuming man always clad in a worn sweatshirt, glasses and brown work pants."

Frogs #1. 43" x 30". By George Wilson, Oakland, California. 2005. "A quiet yet fast-paced man, George Wilson has a cup of coffee before he starts each studio day. George's nearly frantic pace when drawing with Prismacolor Stix creates a saturation of color that blends both figure and background. George's rug designs exude strength and romance."

Chapter Four

Let's Celebrate

Celebrations, whether honoring the birth of a child, a marriage, or a holiday are a popular theme when creating rugs. They have even been the theme of an entire exhibit.

Celebrate Life
An American/Japanese Exhibit

In 2000, two fiber artists, Marilyn Bottjer and Kei Koyayashi, decided to co-curate an international rug hooking exhibit. Shown in New York City, New York and Tokyo, Japan, the exhibit was seen by thousands of people. It was the hope of Marilyn and Kei that the exhibit would increase awareness of the beauty of rug hooking.

Forty-four pieces were featured, twenty American and twenty-four Japanese. The artists were asked to limit the size of their pieces to no more than 24" x 24", because the exhibit had to be shipped back and forth between the USA and Japan. This exhibit traveled for one year.

Photography by Erma C. Estwick.

Mooie, the Christmas Angel. 18" x 22". By Mary Raymond Alenstein, Briarcliff Manor, New York. 2000. In Mary's family, the person who hands out presents on Christmas morning is called the Christmas Angel. The first Christmas after her mother's death was a sad time and no one felt like handing out the presents. Secretly, Mary's daughter Abby dressed her cow hand puppet Mooie in a halo and white wings made of paper plates. On Christmas morning the puppet appeared on Abby's hand to give out the presents. Laughter erupted and somehow the lingering sadness disappeared, thanks to Mooie, the secret angel.

Fourth of July, New York City. 11" x 18". By Marilyn Bottjer, Eastchester, New York. 2000. There seems to be nothing more celebratory than Fourth of July fireworks over the East River presented to the city of New York by Macy's Department Store. Thousands of onlookers crowd the area to see the sky lit by fireworks in celebration of Independence Day.

No Braver Soul Than I. 23" x 20". By Linda Rae Coughlin, Warren, New Jersey. 2000. This piece celebrates the gift of life that is given to each of us. This life must be embraced fully and faced without fear. For some, it isn't until they are faced with a challenge, whether it be physical, emotional, or spiritual, that they truly begin to appreciate this precious thing we call life.

Party Animal. 21" x 21". By Gail Dufresne, Lambertville, New Jersey. 2000. When asked to create a celebratory rug, Gail designed the monitor lizard playing a saxophone and wearing a party hat. New Year's Eve, especially since it rang in the new millennium, seemed the perfect occasion.

Celebration of Living. 19" x 24". By Ann Erskine, Ridgefield, Connecticut. 2000. Reminding Ann of the passage of time, seasonal flowers were used to represent the cycle of life. Birth is symbolized by the spring, Viola Adorata; youth by the summer, Clematis; adulthood is shown by the autumn, Aster; and maturity by the winter, Hellebore.

Wednesday Night Races. 12" x 24". By Gail H. Horton, Greenport, New York. 2000. It is a longstanding tradition that people who live in a seaside community go to roads' ends on the water to check out what the sea tells them about the days ahead. This piece is a view from the road on a Wednesday evening in late summer. As the sun sets at the end of a long day, Gail's husband watches the conclusion of a sailboat race as her son's tugboat, "The Patricia Gail," eases into its mooring in the creek.

The Ann and Peg Show. 22" x 20". By Peg Irish, Waquoit, Massachusetts. 2000. Rug hooking promotes friendships that unite people around the globe. When Peg moved away from her friend Ann, she could no longer hook side-by-side with her. This piece is a tribute to her friendship with Ann Winterling.

Labor Day Weekend at the Farm. 23" x 17". By Laurie Ling, Croton, New York. 2000. This rug shows the countless Labor Day weekends Laurie spent as a child on the family farm in southern Vermont. She has fond memories of those days and now enjoys spending time there with her own and extended family.

Celebration Birthday. 18" x 18". By Roslyn Logsdon, Bethesda, Maryland. 1999. Roslyn writes, "Because birthdays are a special time, I am lucky to share my birthday with a dear friend. Since our birthdays are two days apart we celebrate together, opening presents and then going someplace special with our husbands. This rug shows Karen blowing out the candles, as I share in our birthday cake on a summer afternoon."

Southwest Desert. 27" x 15". By Maggie McLea, Glastonbury, Connecticut. 1999. "This work is in celebration of the hours and days I spent sketching and learning to love the southwestern desert. It is anything but drab, dull, or dreary."

Trick or Treat. 23" x 20". By Pat Merikallio, Capitola, California. 2000. "I've always loved Halloween because it really is mostly for children, and it was a day that my children loved almost more than Christmas. They loved making their own costumes and, of course, they especially loved the candy they collected for 'trick or treat.'"

Christmas Fox. 15" x 20". By Betty Oberstar, Wilton, Connecticut. 2000. After seeing two foxes silhouetted against snow in her yard, Betty decided to hook an imaginary fox by a tree in her front yard at Christmas time.

Groundhog Day. 25" x 19". By June Myles, Redding, Connecticut. 2000. "Groundhog Day, coming as it does on February 2nd, is the first harbinger of spring. So, it celebrates hope! If Punxsutawney Phil sees his shadow, there will be six more weeks of winter. Though often a poor weather prognosticator, it's wonderful to think that spring is just around the corner. It is also one of the few non-commercialized holidays left."

Graduation. 24" x 24". By Emily K. Robertson, Falmouth, Massachusetts. 2000. "Graduation represents the conclusion of one part of life and the beginning of another, the completion of formal studies and the emergence of the graduate into the 'real world.' This change can be daunting or it can be fun."

Anniversary. 14" x 19". By Olga Rothschild, Duxbury, Massachusetts. 2000. "This is a schematic of Michael and Kristin Hemming's 15th anniversary. They are in Japanese kimonos because that is what they gave us as a wedding present. The decoration around the edge is folksy. Kristin is Norwegian. The score card - 15 - is for Michael's love of games and gambling. The red, green, and gray colors are from their old plaid shirts."

Thanksgiving Parade. 24" x 24". By Alice Rudell, New York City, New York. 2000. "Each year the Thanksgiving parade passes by Alice's New York City apartment. Rain or shine, the day is always wonderful with the marching bands, colorful floats, balloons, and crowds of people. All on the somber gray asphalt and skyscraper stage."

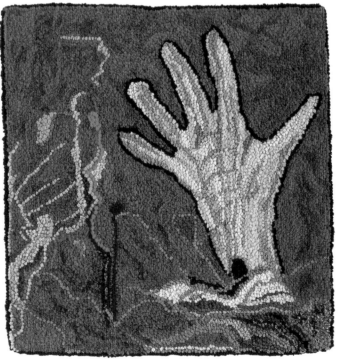

Hope. 12" x 12". By Susan L. Smidt, Salem, Massachusetts. 2000. "The hand in this rug represents my looking forward to a new future after a divorce."

Winter Solstice. 21" x 21". By Jule Marie Smith, Ballston Spa, New York. 2000. "Winter Solstice celebrates the return of the sun represented by the Yule log. Yule means 'wheel.' *Waes Hael* is Celtic for 'Be whole or hale,' hence 'wassail.' The druids gathered mistletoe. Oak overcomes holly. Ivy is a solstice symbol. The deer is Jule Marie's symbol."

Times Square. 23" x 20". By Joan Stocker, Kittery Point, Maine. 2000. Times Square is a place that people from all over the world recognize, and was the place to be on New Years Eve 2000.

Becoming 40. 22" x 22". By Cindy Spence, Saratoga Springs, New York. 2000. This piece represents Cindy's feelings on her fortieth birthday.

The Last Launching Ceremony. 16" x 16". By Hiroshi Ariyoshi, Yokohama, Kanagawa, Japan. 2000. Bottles of champagne, tapes, and fireworks. The shipbuilding yard is being closed after ninety years, a somewhat sentimental moment for workers there.

Boy's Day - A Carp Streamer. 23" x 20". By Mitsue Fukuda, Chiba, Japan. 2000. Carp going against the rapid stream. Wishing for boys to be healthy and full of spirit.

Summer Festival. 20" x 23". By Kumiko Fujita, Saitama, Japan. 2000. One of the traditional festivals in Japan.

Fireworks - Summer Festival. 24" x 19". By Setsuko Fukuda, Tokyo, Japan. 2000. A colorful event to cool off the heat.

A Family Tree. 24" x 24". By Miharu Fuwa, Tokyo, Japan. 2000. Dad, mom, and baby.

Journey Through the USA. 23" x 23". By Kazuko Kaneko, Chiba, Japan. 2000. The melting pot of people from all over the world.

Birthday Celebration. 23" x 20". By Fuka Hiraoka, Toyko, Japan. 2000. The first grandchildren, twins!

Koinobori - Carp Streamers. By Hiromi Murata, Hiromi Sakamoto, Takiko Kawama, Tokyo, Japan. 2000. Three flags for the children of the world.

Image of Japan - A Stone Jizo. 24" x 19". By Eriko Keino, Tokyo, Japan. 2000. A guardian deity for children, standing by the country roadside.

My Dream - Flying to New York. 24" x 24". By Kazuko Kobayashi, Tokyo, Japan. 2000. Celebrating the show in New York.

Aomori Nebuta Festival. 24" x 24". By Shizuko Kimura, Tokyo, Japan. 2000. This festival is held in the northeastern district of Japan and radiates strong passion during the short summer.

A Celebration of American Ingenuity. 23" x 19". By Kei Kobayashi, New York City, New York. 2000. "Blowing my trumpet to Japan, it echoes back, here we are!"

My Family. 24" x 24". By Harumi Matsui, Yokahama, Japan. 2000. This rug shows all the animals Harumi rescued from the streets and made part of her family.

Four Seasons in Japan. 22" x 24". By Noriko Mizuno, Matudo, Japan. 2000. Four seasons designed from a traditional Japanese playing card.

Welcome to Our Family: 1st Year Anniversary. 18" x 24". By Tomoka Miyamoto, Ibarki, Japan. 2000. This rug was made for a squirrel named Chip who joined Tomaka's family.

A Family Trip. 18" x 24". By Haruyo Murata, Tokyo, Japan. 2000. A wonderful trip with time spent together sharing the same air and sun.

Cherry Blossoms. 17" x 23". By Madaka Nagumo, Kanagawa, Japan. 2000. Sukura, the national flower of Japan. Waiting for spring when everyone gets happy.

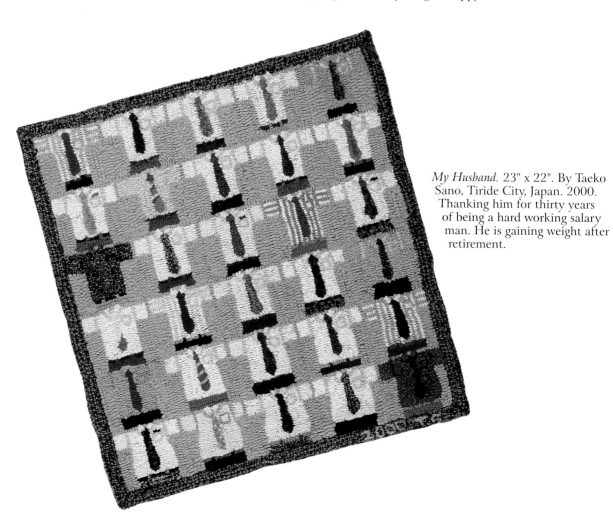

My Husband. 23" x 22". By Taeko Sano, Tiride City, Japan. 2000. Thanking him for thirty years of being a hard working salary man. He is gaining weight after retirement.

My Vision for the 21st Century. 19" x 18". By Hiroko Sato, Ibaragi, Japan. 2000. Hiroko's idea for the universe, a journey into the unknown.

Greetings From Animals. 19" x 23". By Sachiko Toyoda, Kanagawa, Japan. 2000. Designed after seeing animals at the Bronx Zoo.

The Harvest Moon. 24" x 24". By Nobuko Sato, Nagoya, Japan. 2000. In Japan, the harvest moon is celebrated on the nights of September 15th and October 13th, with offerings of fruits and vegetables from the fall harvest.

A Chorus Concert. 16" x 24". By Mutsumi Yamamoto, Tokyo, Japan. 2000. Mitsumi's son is a conductor and won 1st prize. She is a proud mother.

Birth Rugs by Alice Rudell

Over the years, Alice Rudell has created many birth and celebration rugs for her family and friends. Her rugs always tell a story and are wonderful ways for new children in the family to learn a small part of their family history. Shown here are some of the many birth rugs she created over the years. Lucky are the family and friends who receive one of these wonderful pieces of art.

Photography courtesy of Alice Rudell.

Owen's Rug. 29" x 46". By Alice Rudell, New York City, New York. 1998. "Made for the birth of my grandnephew Owen. There are three masts. Each mast carries the initial for the three siblings, 'N' is for Nicholas, 'C' is for Claire and 'O' is for Owen."

Claire's Rug. 24" x 38". By Alice Rudell, New York City, New York. 1993. "This is the first rug made for the birth of my grandniece Claire. Joe was their Dalmatian and Oslo was my dog."

Charlie's Rug. 30" x 47". By Alice Rudell, New York City, New York. 1999. "Made for the birth of my grandniece Charlie, born on Valentine's Day. Hooking the snow was an interesting task."

Jenni's Rug. 30" x 41". By Alice Rudell, New York City, New York. 1996. "Made for the birth of my grandniece Jenni. The 'D' in the upper left-hand corner is for Daryl, the older sister. The 'J' in the upper right-hand corner stands for Jake, the older brother."

> *Art parallels life. Capture your passion in your rugs.*

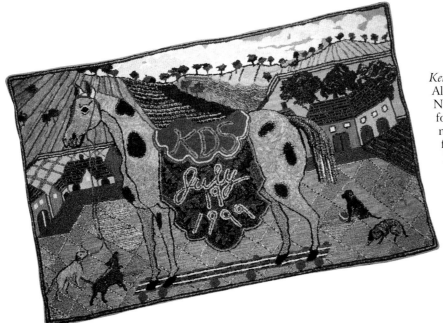

Kenny's Rug. 30" x 47". By Alice Rudell, New York City, New York. 1999. "Made for the birth of my grand-nephew Kenny, born into a family of horse lovers. This horse is on wheels."

Zack's Rug. 47" x 30". By Alice Rudell, New York City, New York. 1997. "Made for the birth of my grandnephew Zack. His older brother is Kenny."

Reece's Rug. 44" x 28". By Alice Rudell, New York City, New York. 2004. "Made for the birth of my grand-niece Reece. The pretty dog holding the cute baby in a basket is Lucy, the family's English Mastiff."

Other Celebration Rugs

Included here are some other playful examples of rugs hooked with a celebration theme.

Ohio Bi-Centennial Horse. 18" x 24". By Carole K. Bartolovich, Avon, Ohio. 2003. After seeing this at an antique show (rocking horse in front of "Ohio Star Quilt") Carole bought the horse, made the quilt, hooked the rug. *Courtesy of Carole Bartolovich.*

Tyler's Rug. 18" x 24". By Susan Andreson, Newport Beach, California. 2003. Made to commemorate the birth of Cheat and his wife Linda's first grandchild. *Courtesy of Susan Andreson.*

WWI. 22" x 30". By Carole K. Bartolovich, Avon, Ohio. 2001. "Commemorative rug honoring my great uncle, L.Z. Phillips, who wrote the 'Marine's Hymn.'" (Medals and memo are attached to the rug.) *Courtesy of Carole Bartolovich.*

Independence Day. 22" x 28". By Carole K. Bartolovich, Avon, Ohio. 2003. "My grandchildren by the sea." *Courtesy of Carole Bartolovich.*

Marriage Portrait. 26" x 22". By Margaret Lutz, Flemington, New Jersey. 1994. *Photography by Linda Rae Coughlin.*

The Engaged Couple. 40" x 42". By Emily K. Robertson, Falmouth, Massachusetts. 1995. "The photograph that inspired this rug hung on my refrigerator for a few months while I enjoyed the patterns of the books and the antique afghan as well as the similarities in the sweater colors of my daughter, Chris and her then fiancé, Neal. One morning it all came together to become a rug pattern. I am so pleased that the finished piece has held a place of prominence in Chris and Neal's home." *Photography by Diane Marshall.*

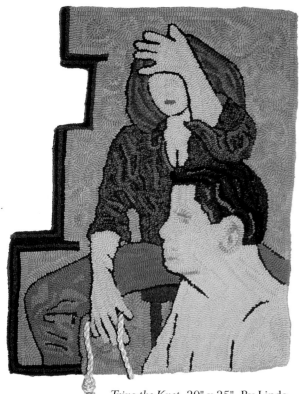

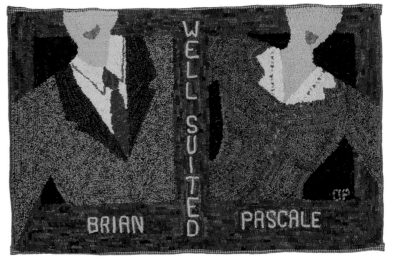

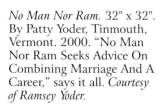

Tying the Knot. 20" x 25". By Linda Rae Coughlin, Warren, New Jersey. 2004. This piece looks at what the meaning of the phrase "tying the knot" might be. *Photography by Linda Rae Coughlin.*

Well Suited. 32" x 50". By Deanie Pass, Minneapolis, Minnesota. 2004. "Created for my stepson Brian and his wife Pascale for their 15th wedding anniversary. Brian is a lawyer, a 'suit' in today's jargon, and Pascale is his fashionable French wife, who creates and sells wonderful necklaces. So it was an obvious image." *Courtesy of Deanie Pass.*

No Man Nor Ram. 32" x 32". By Patty Yoder, Tinmouth, Vermont. 2000. "No Man Nor Ram Seeks Advice On Combining Marriage And A Career," says it all. *Courtesy of Ramsey Yoder.*

The Wedding Rug. 33" x 39". By Emily K. Robertson, Falmouth, Massachusetts. 1998. "The saying on this rug is of African origin and my husband, Mike, and I felt that it captured the optimism and hope that we had as we entered into our new life adventure together. The hands are our own in every imaginary way of joining to signify the work that we planned to do together." *Photography by Diane Marshall.*

After Uncle Andy's Wedding. 22" x 37". By Debbie Walsh, Cranford, New Jersey. 2004. "My three children were in their uncle's wedding in Vermont. Eric changed out of his suit and tie, but Devin and Maggie still had on their dresses when I snapped this shot of them." *Courtesy of Debbie Walsh.*

Wedding Rug. 28" x 40". By Lyle Drier, Waukesha, Wisconsin. 1998. "I designed this rug along with my mother, Florence Dressler, in honor of my youngest sister's wedding. My mom was the architect, while I was the gardener." *Courtesy of Lyle Drier.*

Vermont Celebration. 29" x 36". By Gail Ferdinando and Debbie Walsh, Pittstown and Cranford, New Jersey. "Made to commemorate Father's 70th birthday. The two sisters, brother, and father (in hat) are sitting on rocks at a Vermont pond." *Courtesy of Debbie Walsh.*

Alek's Birth Rug. 39" x 40". By Emily K. Robertson, Falmouth, Massachusetts. 2005. "Here is a rug that can teach my grandson about his ancestry should he ever inquire. Alek's family name, Erickson, is Swedish and my son wanted to commemorate this proud heritage. However, apart from Alek's name, his origins are mostly English. I used the Runic alphabet for Alek's name and my initials, but the imagery came from the Bayeux Tapestry commemorating the Norman Invasion of England. The symbols are Celtic. The purple horse on the ship is for Alek's sister, Abby, who loves horses and purple." *Photography by Diane Marshall.*

Island Life. 33" x 22". By Elizabeth Williamson, Severna, Maryland. 2005. The theme of this wedding present was to capture the uniqueness of this couple's growing up, marrying, and living only on islands. The islands are: Manhattan, Staten Island, Long Island, Shelter Island, and Jamaica. *Courtesy of Elizabeth Williamson.*

Bernie's 40th Birthday. 34" x 28". By Patti Ann Finch, Medford, New Jersey. 2003. *Courtesy of Patti Ann Finch.*

Spirit of America Take Flight. 30" x 30". By Joyce Krueger, Waukesha, Wisconsin. 1989. Inspired by the folk art show "Spirit of America Take Flight." The challenge was to design a piece of art in your own art medium that reflected the show. *Courtesy of Joyce Krueger.*

Liberty. 32" x 25". By Joyce Krueger, Waukesha, Wisconsin. 2000. "I design a holiday rug each year. This is my July 4th rug." *Courtesy of Joyce Krueger.*

No Calorie Easter Basket. 16" x 18". By Patti Ann Finch, Medford, New Jersey. 2004. *Courtesy of Patti Ann Finch.*

Thanksgiving Memory. 30" x 44". By Alice Rudell, New York City, New York. 1995. "We always have the whole family for Thanksgiving. This rug depicts my husband's mastery of carving the turkey. Everyone born before 1995 is included—pets as well." *Courtesy of Alice Rudell.*

Bag Full of Goodies. 19" x 30". By Margaret Dickerson, Point Pleasant Beach, New Jersey. 2000. Father Christmas in his flowing robe. Rope and cap tassels are raised hooking. *Photography by Linda Rae Coughlin.*

Chapter Five

A Reflection of Oneself and Others

The human body is always a fascinating and challenging subject for creating art. This section features some wonderful pieces having to do with the self and others.

The Many Faces of Linda Friedman Schmidt

Self-taught fiber artist Linda Friedman Schmidt has created this series of portrait and figurative expressionist fiber paintings with discarded clothing and even, occasionally, plastic bags. Of her work, Linda writes:

Portraiture enables me to discover who I am, to explore the emotional and psychological impact of my life experiences. Through figurative art, I respond to life, I express the real me. I see myself in the faces of others, I see our common humanity. All of the people in my work are me.

Portraits are linked to identity and self-awareness. My parents tried to change my identity. A false self emerged because I was so exquisitely tuned to their expectations. I grew up uncomfortable in my own skin.

My medium, discarded clothing, represents the "second skin." The skin is the sign of our transformability, our ability to become other, and yet to persist and survive in that becoming other. Looking at the notion that clothes make the person, or you are what you wear, I deconstruct what I have been wearing, layers of psychological trauma, and transform them to create a new identity—the person I want to be, the real me.

I was clothed in sadness. The discarded clothing transformed is the sad life discarded and reinvented. I shed and transform the layers to reveal my true, joyous identity. As I hand cut each strip, I experience the pleasure of cutting what I no longer need from my life.

Discarded clothes are remnants, displaced, odd pieces, leftovers. I was born in Germany in a Displaced Person's Camp. I am rescuing my family and myself (biblical reference "holy remnants") with this work.

The hand-cut strips of discarded clothing can also represent lint, something that sticks to you, hard to get rid of, unwanted, like the pain from emotional suffering. I am driven to transform that lint, that emotional pain, into beauty.

Lint is passed from person to person through incidental contact. It is a way to connect with others, an opportunity for exchange. There was little emotional connection in my war-traumatized family. Growing up, I felt like an outsider, different, yet I yearned for a connection with others. Now, I brush up against countless others whose clothing wears on, and whose faces appear in my work.

I am piecing together and repairing the fabric of my life. I am condensing old clothes, photographs, images in my head, and a lifetime of feelings. I am putting together the pieces that make up the patterns of my soul, coming to know who I am. I am cutting out the old, sad story and creating a more pleasing, colorful one.

I am transforming women's work into something new, whose whole is greater than the sum of its parts, transforming the ordinary into the extraordinary, transforming sadness into gladness. I give new meaning to the idea of fashion as art.

My work is a celebration of color, texture, and handwork. There is joy, peace and love in the process of creation. This is my spiritual journey, immersed in every detail, experiencing the pleasure of the now, the hands working and moving in a steady rhythm, the rhythm of life.

Photography courtesy of Linda Friedman Schmidt.

The human body is one of my favorite subjects when it comes to creating my own art. I hope you enjoy the amazing pieces that were created using the self and others as the subject matter.

Looking Good, Feeling Bad. 43" x 29". By Linda Friedman Schmidt, Franklin Lakes, New Jersey. 1999.

Mask. 52" x 35". By Linda Friedman Schmidt, Franklin Lakes, New Jersey. 2000.

Stifled Sisters. 58" x 38". By Linda Friedman Schmidt, Franklin Lakes, New Jersey. 2000.

Can't Reach the Joy. 40" x 35". By Linda Friedman Schmidt, Franklin Lakes, New Jersey. 2000.

Salsa Cures Sadness. 60" x 42". By Linda Friedman Schmidt, Franklin Lakes, New Jersey. 2002.

No More Scars. 59" x 36". By Linda Friedman Schmidt, Franklin Lakes, New Jersey. 2001. Detail.

Dance of Hope and Despair. 60" x 40". By Linda Friedman Schmidt, Franklin Lakes, New Jersey. 2002.

Plastic Fantastic Makeover. 68" x 44". By Linda Friedman Schmidt, Franklin Lakes, New Jersey. 2003. Detail #2.

Plastic Fantastic Makeover. 68" x 44". By Linda Friedman Schmidt, Franklin Lakes, New Jersey. 2003. Detail #1.

Ben - Woe is He. 11" x 9". By Linda Friedman Schmidt,
Franklin Lakes, New Jersey. 2003.

Displaced Citizen. 11" x 12". By Linda
Friedman Schmidt, Franklin Lakes, New
Jersey. 2003. Detail.

Helen Loved Flowers. 11" x 9". By Linda Friedman Schmidt,
Franklin Lakes, New Jersey. 2003.

When Mother Can't Mother. 63" x 41". By Linda Friedman Schmidt, Franklin Lakes, New Jersey. 2003. Detail.

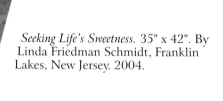

Never Too Late. 12" x 12". By Linda Friedman Schmidt, Franklin Lakes, New Jersey. 2003.

Seeking Life's Sweetness. 35" x 42". By Linda Friedman Schmidt, Franklin Lakes, New Jersey. 2004.

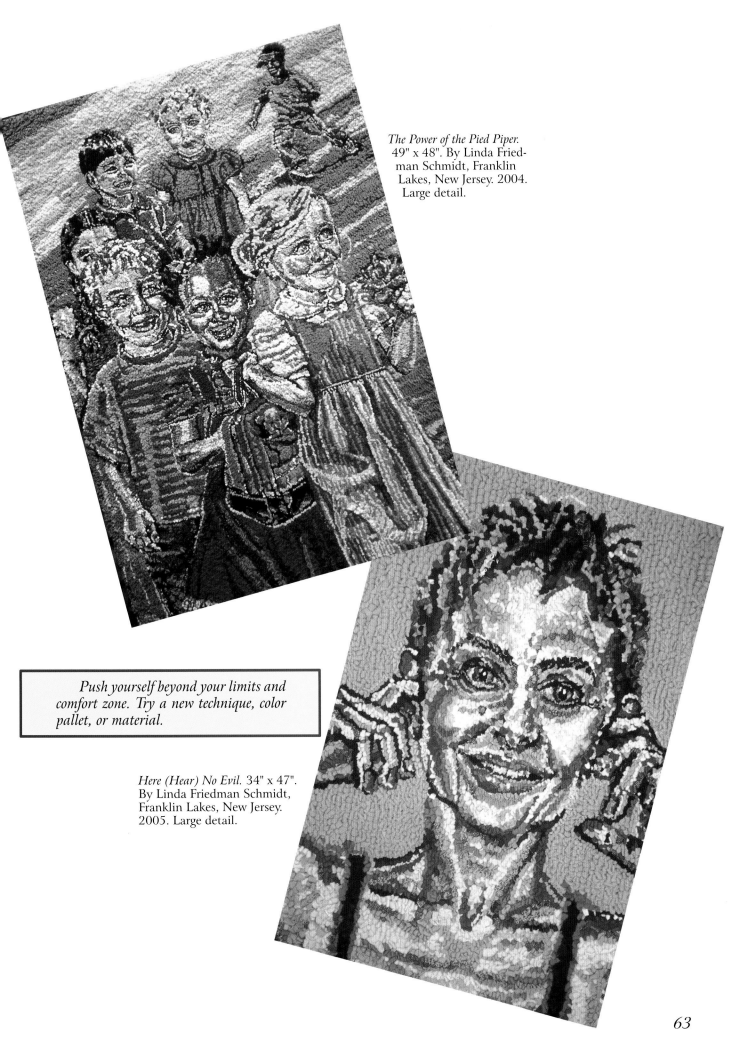

The Power of the Pied Piper.
49" x 48". By Linda Friedman Schmidt, Franklin
Lakes, New Jersey. 2004.
Large detail.

*Push yourself beyond your limits and
comfort zone. Try a new technique, color
pallet, or material.*

Here (Hear) No Evil. 34" x 47".
By Linda Friedman Schmidt,
Franklin Lakes, New Jersey.
2005. Large detail.

Local Folks by Deanne Fitzpatrick

Fiber artist Deanne Fitzpatrick has an enormous body of work that follows a common theme of family and friends in rural Nova Scotia, Canada. She writes about her figurative series:

When I hook people, I am more interested in getting the feeling of them than in what they actually look like. I want to create a sense of them as people. I use their clothing and their movement as a method of expressing themselves. I do not hook the faces in for a few reasons. I like it that they could be anyone, that they are a soul, rather than an individual. Secondly, I hook in a primitive style with wide cuts of cloth and the medium does not allow you to show this sort of detail. Thus my people are more impressionistic than realistic.

I am interested in portraits of everyday people, particularly those in common activities. Often their story is told by what they are holding in their hand. I am interested in rural life and working people because this is what I know and understand. I grew up with it and am accustomed to it. I am comfortable with it.

I really like to create images of domestic life. My mother was a housewife. As a child I would watch her wipe down the counter, make the bread, and sweep the floor all day. At night she would don her bandana and camel hair coat and go off to bingo. My own life holds plenty of domesticity, though thankfully little bingo. Once I resented domesticity, now I take pleasure in it, knowing that it is a privilege to be able to be young, in good health, and able to care for others. That is

not to say I do not tire of it and wish to be the woman in the blue dress, for everyone must wish for this at one time or another. I enjoy domestic images and believe that in carrying out these simple things we create a life with one another, and build a time together.

My rugs are sometimes stories, and sometimes they are just images that have developed in my head. They have popped up out of nowhere, or from a picture or a person I've come across. Sometimes I do not know their stories but as I hook them I invent stories for them. Once a man came to the studio to buy a rug for his wife. He wanted an image of a village or a pretty scene, which I often do. This was right before a show I was having called The Common Soul, which was a body of portraiture of everyday people. The studio walls were filled with these rugs. When he came in he said, "My god, they almost scare me, the people in these mats seem half alive." The people all over the walls bothered him; they made him slightly uncomfortable. His discomfort did not bother me because that is what I want. I want these imaginary figures to make people feel something, and anything they feel is fine with me.

The people in my rugs are people I know. My mother emerges again and again, so does my childhood next-door neighbor, Mr. Bernie. I often see my sisters in the dancing girls just the way they were when, as a little girl, I was watching them get ready to go out on a Saturday night. All of the people I hook are familiar to me in one way or another. I enjoy their company.

Photography courtesy of Deanne Fitzpatrick.

Washing on the River Bank. 54" x 40". By Deanne Fitzpatrick, Amherst, Nova Scotia, Canada. 2005.

Meaning of the Journey. 54" x 48". By Deanne Fitz-patrick, Amherst, Nova Scotia, Canada. 2001.

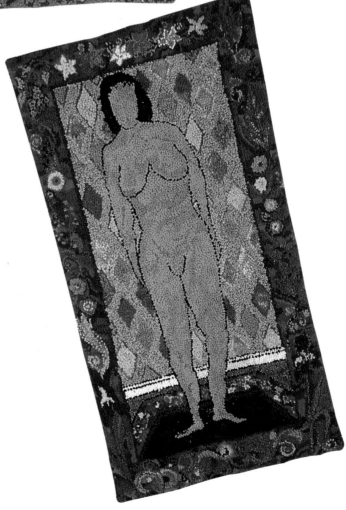

Common Soul. 78" x 56". By Deanne Fitzpatrick, Amherst, Nova Scotia, Canada. 2000. Four separate pieces that each measure 78" x 14".

Standing Naked on the Mat. 54" x 38". By Deanne Fitzpatrick, Amherst, Nova Scotia, Canada. 2003.

Picking Potatoes. 36" x 78". By Deanne Fitzpatrick, Amherst, Nova Scotia, Canada. 2005.

Woman on the Path. 42" x 32". By Deanne Fitzpatrick, Amherst, Nova Scotia, Canada. 2004.

Standing on the Bog. 66" x 54". By Deanne Fitzpatrick, Amherst, Nova Scotia, Canada. 2004.

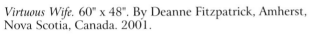

Virtuous Wife. 60" x 48". By Deanne Fitzpatrick, Amherst, Nova Scotia, Canada. 2001.

Fish in Hand. 50" x 16". By Deanne Fitzpatrick, Amherst, Nova Scotia, Canada. 2002.

Woman in a Blue Dress. 66" x 36". By Deanne Fitzpatrick, Amherst, Nova Scotia, Canada. 2005.

Other Portraits

Other examples of some of the many amazing portraits being created.

Head Games. 31" x 38". By Donna Lee Beaudoin, Hinesburg, Vermont. 2005. A man with a leaf in his hair, a woman with a flower. *Photography by Linda Rae Coughlin.*

IDA. 19" x 13". By Burma Cassidy, Rochester, Vermont. 2005. Mixed Fiber *Courtesy of Burma Cassidy.*

Earth From Above. 47" x 43". By Burma Cassidy, Rochester, Vermont. 2005. A self-portrait. *Courtesy of Burma Cassidy.*

Beauty. 16" x 11". By Nola Heidbreder, St. Louis, Missouri. 2005. Portrait of a woman. *Courtesy of Nola Heidbreder.*

Mirror, Mirror. 16" x 15". By Peg Irish, Waquoit, Massachusetts. 2002. "Mirror, mirror, how can it be, that old woman, she is me." *Courtesy of Peg Irish.*

A Head Above the Rest. 30" x 24". By Peg Irish, Waquoit, Massachusetts. 1999. Portrait of Peg's husband. *Courtesy of Peg Irish.*

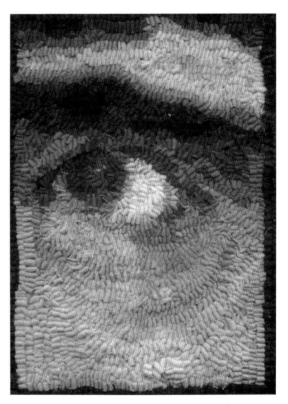

Connection. 8" x 6". By Mary Klotz, Woodsboro, Maryland. 2006. This image of a young man's eye was worked three times, once as a painting in 1999, once as a triaxial weaving in 2002, and finally as a hooked piece in 2006, which was then made into a pillow. Mary notes that she is still not finished with the image and is working on two more pieces. *Courtesy of Mary Klotz.*

Self Portrait with Pendleton and Pups. 42" x 26". By Mary Logue, Golden Valley, Minnesota. 2004. The artist used only recycled and naturally dyed wools. *Courtesy of Mary Logue.*

When She Knew Everything. 24" x 23". By Susan Marks, Madison, Wisconsin. 2004. "This piece was inspired by a photo of myself taken when I was in my thirties and was spunky and thought I knew everything." *Courtesy of Susan Marks.*

Engaging Love. 14" x 20". By Angela Mork, West Allis, Wisconsin. 2001. Designed by Angela's husband Nicholas. *Courtesy of Angela Mork.*

Amelia. 12" x 12". By Jule Marie Smith, Ballston Spa, New York. 2005. Study in complementary colors and the look of dawn and wind blown sky. *Courtesy of Jule Marie Smith.*

Allumina. 12" x 12". By Jule Marie Smith, Ballston Spa, New York. 2005. A woman seemingly trapped in an onion. *Courtesy of Jule Marie Smith.*

Going to Pieces, Getting it Together. 39" x 24". By Sharon L. Townsend, Altoona, Iowa. 2004. A hooked puzzle with nine pieces. *Courtesy of Sharon L. Townsend.*

You Can't Hide. 18" x 14". By Sharon L. Townsend, Altoona, Iowa. 2005. "Life has to be faced." *Courtesy of Sharon L. Townsend.*

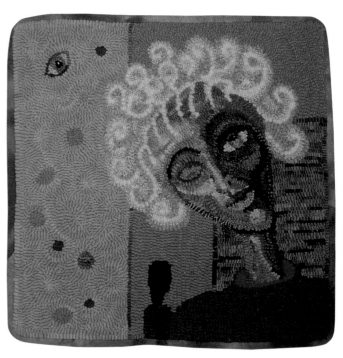

Where Did I Go. 18" x 18". By Sharon L. Townsend, Altoona, Iowa. Inspired by a Modigliani painting, this is a portrait of Sharon's mother, who has dementia and is losing her memory bit by bit. *Courtesy of Sharon L. Townsend.*

Checking the Corners. 15" x 14". By Sharon L. Townsend, Altoona, Iowa. 2005. "Often what you're looking for is too close to find." *Courtesy of Sharon L. Townsend.*

Emma. 48" x 36". By Patty Yoder, Tinmouth, Vermont. 2005. This piece was the last rug completed by Patty. *Photography by Linda Rae Coughlin.*

Notice the subtle royal blue profile of a face that appears in the top left corner of this piece.

Chapter Six

Our Family and Friends

When it comes to subject matter, our family and friends mean so much to us and are a perfect source of inspiration for our art.

Friendship Rugs by the Cream City Hookers

Friendship rugs are a way for a group of friends to work on a project jointly. These rugs were created by the Cream City Hookers ATHA Guild of Milwaukee, Wisconsin. Each rug in the series was created by multiple individuals hooking a portion of a friend's rug—upon completion, everyone then possesses a rug that each friend worked on. Shown here are some very clever ways of doing friendship rugs.

Friendship Rug. 28" x 30". By Ann Rudolph, Wauwatosa, Wisconsin. 2004. Sixteen squares each made by a different guild member in a design around the guild logo. *Courtesy of Ann Rudolph.*

Garden Friendship Rug. 44" x 20". By Hazel Rooker, Watertown, Wisconsin. 2004. Arched flower rug with sun and the toad. *Courtesy of Hazel Rooker.*

Friendship Rug. 20" x 28". By Sally Kraimer, Wauwatosa, Wisconsin. 2003. "Cream City Rug Hookers." *Courtesy of Sally Kraimer.*

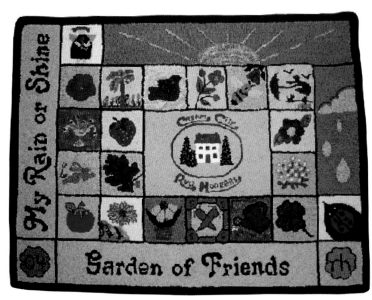

My Rain or Shine Garden of Friends. 25" x 26". By Nancy A. Harland, Waukesha, Wisconsin. 2004. Rain clouds and sun shining with Cream City logo in center. *Courtesy of Nancy A. Harland.*

Friendship Rug. By Marilyn Denning, Burlington, Wisconsin. 2003. Combination of penny rug style, lambs' tongues, and traditional hooking, 36" round. *Courtesy of Marilyn Denning.*

Sunflower Friendship Rug. By Kay Wachowiak, Greenfield, Wisconsin. 2003. 39" round with irregular edge. *Courtesy of Kay Wachowiak.*

Welcome to My Garden of Rug Hooking Friends. 29" x 30". By Joyce Krueger, Waukesha, Wisconsin. 2004. Weathervane with girl, umbrella, and dog. *Courtesy of Joyce Krueger.*

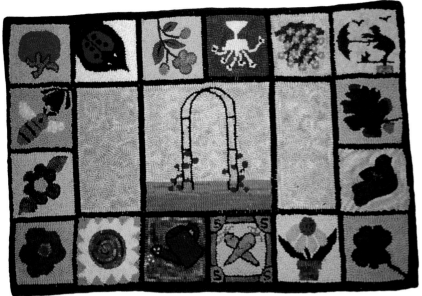

Friendship Rug. 18" x 26". By Kay F.
Porter, Delafield, Wisconsin. 2003.
Flowered arch. *Courtesy of Kay F. Porter.*

Friendship Rug. 20" x 36". By
Lonny Krogman, Sullivan,
Wisconsin. 2004. Sixteen
squares around a friend-
ship border of vines and
insects. *Courtesy of Lonny
Krogman.*

Geranium Friendship Rug. 26" x 23". By
Suzanne Wallner, Oconomowoc, Wiscon-
sin. 2004. Geranium in pot. *Courtesy of
Suzanne Wallner.*

Garden of Rug Hooking Delights. 25" x 36". By Lyle Drier, Waukesha, Wisconsin. 2003. Garden fence surrounds a path of friendship squares. *Courtesy of Lyle Drier.*

Friendship Rug. 27" x 23". By Suzanne Ziegler, Waukesha, Wisconsin. 2004. Twelve squares with four additional squares in corners. Border done in hit or miss green strips. *Courtesy of Suzanne Ziegler.*

Garden Angel. 44" x 47". By Jackie Kojis, Greenfield, Wisconsin. 2003. Angel's flowers worked in wool from each person's square. *Courtesy of Jackie Kojis.*

Friendship Rug. 17" x 25". By Elizabeth E. Williams, Delafield, Wisconsin. 2004. Cream City Rug Hookers logo in center. Twenty four-inch squares surround the logo. *Courtesy of Elizabeth E. Williams.*

Friendship Rug. 25" x 34". By Martha Crawford, Greenfield, Wisconsin. 2003. Friends' initials in center. *Courtesy of Martha Crawford.*

Romance Series by Cecille Caswell

Cecille Caswell of Sherwood Park, Alberta, Canada, did these three pieces on the theme of love. *Photography courtesy of Cecille Caswell.*

> *The use of bold colors sends a strong statement. You can tell so much about a person from the colors they tend to gravitate to.*

Romance - Part 2. 27" x 22". By Cecille Caswell, Sherwood Park, Alberta, Canada. 2004. Colorful depiction of a couple walking along the beach with bright sunset.

Romance - Part 1. 28" x 19". By Cecille Caswell, Sherwood Park, Alberta, Canada. 2004. Colorful depiction of a couple dancing. "Poetry of the heart" hooked along the bottom.

Romance - Part 3. 24" x 19". By Cecille Caswell, Sherwood Park, Alberta, Canada. 2005. Colorful depiction of romantic dinner for two.

Friendship Design Squares - TIGHR 2000

These forty-two Friendship Squares were designed by some of the members of The 2000 International Guild of Handhooking Rugmakers (TIGHR) for their conference, which is held every three years in a different location around the world. In 2000, this conference was held on Cape Cod, Massachusetts. Each member was asked to create an eight-inch square piece that reflected the artist's interest, country, or hooking style. At the end of the conference, these mats were then exchanged among the members in a friendship swap, with each member leaving with a different mat than the one they created.

Photography by Linda Rae Coughlin.

Be a Good Egg. By Marilyn Bottjer, Eastchester, New York.

Red Heart. By Barbara Benner, Cheshire, Oregon.

Mayflower. By Shirley Bradshaw, Yarmouth, Nova Scotia, Canada.

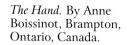

The Hand. By Anne Boissinot, Brampton, Ontario, Canada.

Rosey-Posey. By Lucy Clark, Woodstock, Virginia.

No. By Linda Rae Coughlin, Warren, New Jersey.

Sampler. By Gloria E. Crouse, Olympia, Washington.

Maple Moose. By Barbara D'Arcy, Toronto, Ontario, Canada.

Lady Bug. By Gail Dufresne, Lambertville, New Jersey.

Eucalyptus. By Anne Douglas, Wilson, West Australia, Australia.

A Sculptured Rose for TIGHR. By Ruth Emerson, Grimsby, Ontario, Canada.

Lily. By Jeanne Fallier, Westford, Massachusetts.

Inukshuk. By Jeanne Field, Aurora, Ontario, Canada.

Shofar - The Ram's Horn. By Joan Frankenthal,
Ramat Hasharon, Israel.

Sunflower. By Jan Graham, London, Kentucky.

Cardinal. By Cindy Harpring, Lexington, Kentucky.

2000. By Fumiyo Hachisuka, Tokyo, Japan.

Untitled. By Carol Harvey-Clark, Bridgewater, Nova Scotia, Canada.

Liz. By Peg Irish, Waquoit, Massachusetts.

Ma-ah-ah-th-er-er. By E. Germaine James, Colborne, Ontario, Canada.

Life is Just a Bowl of Cherries. By Carrie Bell Jacobus, Oradell, New Jersey.

Rooster. By Margaret Kenny,
Bradford West Yorkshire,
England.

Jonas. By Maryanne Lincoln, Wrentham, Massachusetts.

The Maryanne. By Maryanne Lincoln, Wrentham,
Massachusetts.

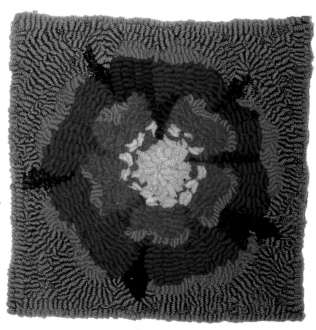

Tudor Rose. By Joan Lindsay, Hullavington, Nr. Chippenham
Wilshire, England.

The Cottage. By Sylvia M. Macdonald, Pictou, Nova Scotia, Canada.

Garden of Seasons - Summer Section. By Sybil Mercer, Southampton, Ontario, Canada.

Nova Scotia. By Mollie "Lee" McBride, Waterville, Nova Scotia, Canada.

Careworn. By Jo-Ann Millen, Boxford, Massachusetts.

Celtic Cat in a Knot. By Doris Norman, Frederickton New Brunswick, Canada.

Good Luck. By Yvonne Muntwyler, Burlington, Ontario, Canada.

Stickley Chair Seat. By Emily K. Robertson, Falmouth, Massachusetts.

Horse Weathervane. By Sandra Robinson, London, Kentucky.

Sunny View. By Iris Simpson, East York, Ontario, Canada.

Jewels. By Olga Rothschild, Duxbury, Massachusetts.

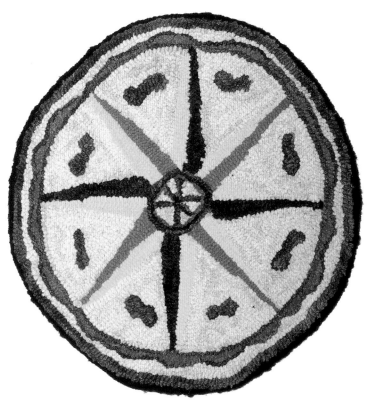

Oh Cat. By Marie "Allene" Thibeault, Provincetown, Massachusetts.

Rain Sun Fertility. By Theresa Strack, Bedford, New Hampshire.

Hobbies. By Laurie M. Sybertz, Kingston, Massachusetts.

Welcome Viking. By Shirley Wiedemann, East Falmouth, Massachusetts.

Mermaid on a Dolphin. By Ann Winterling, Concord, New Hampshire.

Nova Scotia 2000. By Elizabeth Wrathall, Dartmouth, Nova Scotia, Canada.

J is for Josephine. By Patty Yoder, Tinmouth, Vermont.

Family Memories by Sarah Province

Sarah's family has always been a very important part of her life and her art. Over the years, she has created many beautiful hooked pieces documenting her family's history. Each one transports the viewer back to a particular point in time and provides an understanding of what being a part of Sarah's family must have been like. Here she gives us a glimpse of this history as she writes about some of her most vivid family memories:

When we visited my parents at their retirement complex in Richmond, Virginia, they would entertain our elementary school-aged children by showing them old family pictures—scenes from the twenties at the beach in their funny bathing suits, elegant touring cars along with stories of trips with their siblings, and the farm where they grew up, just outside the city limits of Richmond. My first hooking of the series, "Hearthside Memories," was of the fireplace that my father built in our home in North Carolina that they had left, with Mama's blue and white china on the mantle, she hooking a rug before the fire, and Daddy reading the newspaper. It was a deep family memory and I wanted to capture it for always!

After my father had some small strokes, he became depressed and finally had to be moved to the nursing part of their facility. I hooked his grandparents, "Great-Grandma and Great-Grandpa Jones" in front of the home on their sheep farm in Gladys, Virginia. It made him smile and that helped me! "Willow Oaks Farm" was where my mother grew up and, with so many pictures and memories of that historic farmhouse built in 1816, that was my next project.

When one of my daughters moved to California in the early 1990s, I wanted to give her something of home to take with her, so I hooked our home of thirty-five years in Silver Spring, Maryland in the springtime when the azaleas are blooming. Another daughter asked me to hook one of our favorite pictures of my parents, just before they were married in 1926 standing by my dad's Ford Runabout, "Sunday Afternoon, 1926." I started a hooking of my three daughters playing on the beach at Squirrel Island, Maine from a trip that we took when they were young, "All These Things…," and dedicated it to my third daughter. And so the series began!

Now that we are having grandchildren, I am obligated to create a hooking for each of them—"Rosalie's Carousel Ride" is one example. With eight grandchildren, it doesn't look like there will be any end to the series, since, so far, I have completed only four!

Photography courtesy of Sarah Province.

Great-Grandma and Great-Grandpa Jones. 18" x 24". By Sarah Province, Silver Spring, Maryland. 1992. "These are my father's grandparents. Though I didn't know them, my great-grandmother looks very much like my grandmother. My great-grandfather was a sheep farmer."

Hearthside Memories. 24" x 36". By Sarah Province, Silver Spring, Maryland. 1992. "My mother and father sitting by the hearth that my father built with their treasures on it. My mother is hooking a rug and the blue and white English Staffordshire represents her collection."

Willow Oaks Farm. 18" x 24". By Sarah Province, Silver Spring, Maryland. 1993. "This is my mother's home place and the farm on which my father built our home just outside the city limits of Richmond, Virginia. Built in 1816, it was located near a battery of the Civil War and was said to have bullet holes in it from the war."

In a Virginia Garden. 20" x 13". By Sarah Province, Silver Spring, Maryland. 1993. "I found this picture of my paternal grandmother taken in Ashland, Virginia when she was a young girl. It fascinated me to see her in this playful way in such a lovely dress, since I only knew her when she was old and stern."

Two Generations. 20" x 28". By Sarah Province, Silver Spring, Maryland. 1994. "A page from the album of family memories: my mother and her older sister in a photo taken on the boardwalk of Buckroe Beach, Virginia in 1913, and one taken of me in 1948, on the same boardwalk and in the same photo booth, with what looks like almost the same scenery."

Sunday Afternoon 1926. 20" x 15". By Sarah Province, Silver Spring, Maryland. 1996. "My parents shortly before they were married, with my father's 1925 Ford 'Runabout' and in the height of 'flapper fashion.' My mother had 'monkey fur' on her coat and a 20s haircut and curl, rivaling my dad's argyle knee socks, white linen knickers, tweed jacket, and jaunty hat."

My Father and His Sister, Circa 1904. 14" x 12". By Sarah Province, Silver Spring, Maryland. 1997. "I liked this little picture of my father as a baby with his older sister, especially the wicker settee. It is always difficult for me to hook facial features, but I keep trying! My father had restored this gold and white frame so I used it for this piece."

John J. Province, Jr. 12" x 10". By Sarah Province, Silver Spring, Maryland. 1996. "Finding old family photographs often inspires my hooking, as did this one of my husband's brother when he was about three or four years old. I hadn't given up on the wicker yet and also particularly liked his linen suit, the patent-leather shoes, and especially the wooden toy."

Listen to your inner voice. When that inner self wants to take some time to create, let it. Creativity doesn't always happen on our time schedule.

Home in Springtime. 16" x 23". By Sarah Province, Silver Spring, Maryland. 1998. "Our home in Silver Spring, Maryland, located in one of the first suburban developments outside of Washington, D.C. built during the 1920s-30s The whole neighborhood is ablaze with color from the azaleas and dogwoods in the spring."

Harborplace Baltimore. 30" x 36". By Sarah Province, Silver Spring, Maryland. 2002. "When my daughters were teenagers, one of our favorite places to go was Harborplace, especially on Friday evenings. The picture of the three of them on the old anchor was taken on the day the twins graduated from high school at 9:00 in the morning so we spent the day there. Shown collage-style are associated landmarks: in the background are the old power plant, the new aquarium, and the tent shows; closer up is the Bromo-Seltzer Tower; the *Pride of Baltimore II*, with my husband and me; and Camden Yards, noting Cal Ripken #8 up to bat, with my two grandsons, cheering. Black-eyed Susans and the Maryland State flower make up the border."

All These Things... 19" x 25". By Sarah Province, Silver Spring, Maryland. 2001. "A photo taken of my daughters' one vacation in Maine inspired this piece. My young daughter at the water's edge was around the age of four. She was singing a song while looking toward the ocean, one that she had just learned in Sunday School about a boat on the blue sea giving thanks to God for 'all these things you gave to me when you made my eyes to see.'"

How Great Thou Art. 34" x 29". By Sarah Province, Silver Spring, Maryland. 2004. "This scene was taken from our church's Retreat Center overlooking the lake in the fall. The cross, which stands at the front of the outdoor worship area, dominates the scene as it puts Christ in the foreground with God's creation singing in the brilliant colors of the foliage. We often went to Vespers there as a family and one of my daughters was married in the worship center."

Rosalie's Carousel Ride. 25" x 39". By Sarah Province, Silver Spring, Maryland. 2005. "One of my daughters and her family lived in Santa Monica, California for a year, and when we came to visit them, we loved riding on the restored carousel on the world-famous Pier. This piece features Rosalie, my granddaughter, and myself on the glittering carousel, with its gold beads, ribbons, and sequins."

Chapter Seven

Locations of Importance

Where we live or have visited can be of great importance to us and can easily stimulate a wealth of ideas. Look at how many different ways these two series interpret a place of meaning to the artists.

Vermont Vignettes

There are eighty-seven pieces in this collection, all having something to do with the theme "Vermont."

Each piece is horizontal and measures 12" x 14". They were completed as a project for the Green Mountain Rug Hooking Guild and shown at the Guild's 2003 rug exhibit at the Shelburne Museum, Shelburne, Vermont. Following the exhibit, all eighty-seven rugs were shown at the Vermont State House, Montpelier, Vermont.

Photography by Linda Rae Coughlin.

Eye on the Sky. By Nancy Zickler, St. Johnsbury, Vermont.

Rug School. By Diane Phillips, Fairport, New York.

By Cosette Allen, Montpelier, Vermont.

Maple Syrup. By Susan Mackey, Tinmouth, Vermont.

By Alexandra Whitelock, Calais, Vermont.

Autumn in Vermont. By Diane S. Kelly, Dorset, Vermont.

By Francine Oken, Middletown Springs, Vermont.

By Deborah Kelley, Shoreham, Vermont.

By Joan Wheeler, Newport, Vermont.

Green Mountains of Vermont. By Linda Rae Coughlin, Warren, New Jersey.

Snow. By Amy Oxford, Cornwall, Vermont.

By Gail Papetti, Newport Ctr., Vermont.

By Shirley Chaiken, Lebanon, New Hampshire.

In designing a piece, use everyday experiences, a defined focus, a defined color scheme, symbolism, different techniques, and your own uniqueness.

By Diane Burgess, Hinesburg, Vermont.

Autumn in Vermont. By Ann Winterling, Concord,
New Hampshire.

By Bernice Wallman, Granville, New York.

By Betty Bouchard, Richmond, Vermont.

By Grace Hostetter,
Ballston Spa, New York.

By Sue Lawler, Dorset, Vermont.

Cows. By Burma Cassidy, Rochester, Vermont.

Est. 1761 Wallingford. By Elizabeth Morgan, Wallingford, Vermont.

Village Ladies Winter on the Green. By Burma Cassidy, Rochester, Vermont.

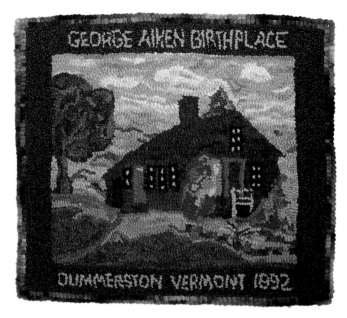

George Aiken's Birth Place. By Jill Aiken, Colchester, Vermont.

Antiques. By Arlene Scanlon, Essex Jct., Vermont.

I'd Jump for a Hump of Cherry Garcia. By Jean
Barber, Burlington, Vermont.

By Anne-Marie W. Littenberg, Burlington, Vermont.

Take Back Vermont. By Joan Mohrmann, Adirondack, New York.

By Eugenie Delaney, N. Ferrisburgh, Vermont.

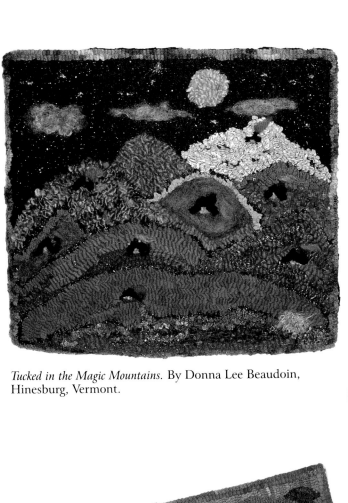

Tucked in the Magic Mountains. By Donna Lee Beaudoin, Hinesburg, Vermont.

By Sue Janssen, Benson, Vermont.

By Helen Mach, Pawlet, Vermont.

Cochron's. By Julie Rogers, Huntington, Vermont.

By Barbara D. Pond, South Burlington, Vermont.

By Phyllis Riley, Greenwich, New York.

Fireworks over Burlington Harbor. By Mary Hulette, South Burlington, Vermont.

A Civil Vermont. By Susan Gingras, Weybridge, Vermont.

Tinker Farm. By Kathy Boozan, So. Burlington, Vermont.

Sugar on Snow. By Joan Hebert, Waterbury Center, Vermont.

Earthquake Shakes Up Rug Hooking Conference. By Peg Irish, Waquoit, Massachusetts.

The Denton House - Jamaica, Vermont. By Joanna Palmer, Melrose, Massachusetts.

By Maureen Yates, So. Burlington, Vermont.

Winter Dreaming. By Cecely Conrad & Stephanie Krauss, Montpelier, Vermont.

Moonlight Ski. By Johanna White, Hinesburg, Vermont.

By Sharon Laufer, Williamstown, Vermont.

Hooked Rug Show. By Kim Dubay, No. Yarmouth, Maine.

By Mary Ellen Von Holt, Marietta, Georgia.

Long Trail. By Mary Sargent, Johnson, Vermont.

Fort Independence 1777. By Judi Brownell, Castleton, Vermont.
Castleton, Vermont.

Our Suzanne. By Jo-Ann Millen, Boxford, Massachusetts.

By Elizabeth Edwards, Williston, Vermont.

Pink Nose Goes to Vermont. By Emily K. Robertson, Falmouth, Massachusetts.

By Dolores Park, Castleton, Vermont.

General Store. By Celia Oliver, Shelburne, Vermont.

By Georgie Abbiati, Montpelier, Vermont.

By Linda Repasky, Amherst,
Massachusetts.

By Cyndi Melendy Labelle, Hinesburg, Vermont.

Brown Swiss. By Laurie M. Sybertz, Kingston, Massachusetts.

By Jule Marie Smith,
Ballston Spa, New York.

By Judy Quintman, Wilmington,
North Carolina.

Ethan Allen Homestead. By Karen T. Martin, Burlington, Vermont.

Barre. By Helen Wolfel, Barre, Vermont.

By Deborah Kelley, Shoreham, Vermont.

Waiting For Spring. By Suzanne Dirmaier, Waterbury Center, Vermont.

Antiques. By Polly Minick, Naples, Florida.

By Andrea Sargent, Johnson, Vermont.

Moonlight Over Vermont. By Willadine Cochran, Jericho, Vermont.

Civil Union. By Rae Reynolds Harrell, Hinesburg, Vermont.

By Ann Hallett, Coldwater, Ontario, Canada.

By Dorothy Danforth, Arlington, Vermont.

Lydia. By Patty Yoder, Tinmouth, Vermont.

Rug School. By Maryanne Lincoln, Wrentham, Massachusetts.

Mud Season. By Davey DeGraff, Hinesburg, Vermont.

Vermont Freedom and Unity. By Ruth Frost, East Montpelier, Vermont.

By Robin Garcia, Calais, Vermont.

By Nancy Bachand, Vergennes, Vermont.

By Priscilla Heininger, Shelburne, Vermont.

By Peggy Stanilonis, Vergennes, Vermont.

By Cecelia K. Toth, New York City, New York.

By Pamela Carter, Bristol, Vermont.

By Shirley H. Zandy, Tinmouth, Vermont.

Lady Slipper Orchid. By Sandy Lincoln, Brandon, Vermont.

Equinox Valley Nursery. By Mary Querques, Burnt Hills, New York.

I Love Vermont. By Lory Doolittle, Mt. Holly, Vermont.

By Karen Quigley, Vergennes, Vermont.

By Loretta Bucceri, Danby, Vermont.

By Carol M. Munson,
Sunderland, Vermont.

By Gail Duclos Lapierre, Shelburne, Vermont.

Hudson Valley Scenes

This collection of rugs featuring scenes from the Hudson Valley began after a group of local artists saw the Vermont Vignettes, which were completed as a group project by the Green Mountain Rug Hooking Guild of Vermont (see previous section). Created between 2004-2005, these pieces were inspired by Croton-on-Hudson, New York, a village located along the shores of the Hudson River. Most of the artists who contributed pieces live in the surrounding area and are therefore familiar with the river and the picturesque valley. Collectively, the rugs are all about the same size, with many created from scenes of the land and riverscapes seen from the artists' own homes. Others show historic landmarks in the Hudson Valley.

Photography by Roya Zarrehparver.

Hudson Morning View. 12" x 14". By Barbara Boll-Ingber, Ossining, New York. 2004.

Shad. 12" x 14". By Marilyn Bottjer, Eastchester, New York. 2004.

View of the Hudson River From Ridgecrest Road in Briarcliff Manor. 12" x 14". By Mary Raymond Alenstein, Briarcliff Manor, New York. 2004.

Old Dutch Church. 12" x 14". By Marilyn Bottjer, Eastchester, New York. 2004.

120

Stoney Point Lighthouse. 12" x 16". By Susan Carson, Croton, New York. 2004.

Hudson River in Winter. 12" x 14". By Kazuko DiCroce, Croton, New York. 2004.

The Whippet on the Hudson River. 12" x 14". By Amy Stoner Cotter, Croton, New York. 2004.

Hudson River View. 12" x 14".
By Qing Fan-Dollinger, Croton,
New York. 2004.

Sunnyside. 12" x 14". By Joyce Kapadia,
Ossining, New York. 2004.

Cow Spotting. 12" x 14". By Laurie
Ling, Croton, New York. 2004.

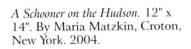

Fish. 12" x 14". By Debra Marrone, Croton, New York. 2005.

A Schooner on the Hudson. 12" x 14". By Maria Matzkin, Croton, New York. 2004.

Van Cortlandt Manor. 12" x 14". By Maria Matzkin, Croton, New York. 2004.

Kitchen Window. 12" x 14". By Nancy Oppedisano, Ossining, New York. 2004.

The Little Red Lighthouse and the Great Gray Bridge. 12" x 14". By Mary Parker, Yorktown Heights, New York. 2004.

The Mohonk Mountain House. 12" x 14". By Mary Parker, Yorktown Heights, New York. 2004.

Looking Up River From West Point. 12" x 14". By Robin Schwamb, Croton, New York. 2004.

On the Hudson at Croton Point. 12" x 14". By Diane R. Skalak, Croton, New York. 2004.

Metro North Train. 12" x 14". By Roya Zarrehparvar, Montrose, New York. 2004.

The Headless Horseman. 12" x 14". By Marian Specter, White Plains, New York. 2004.

Chapter Eight

Playing Cards

Art Rugs: The "Art" of Playing Cards

This is an international hooked rug exhibit that I, Linda Rae, curated to promote the "art" of rug hooking. The idea of Art Rugs is still in its infancy and it is my hope that this and future exhibits will help to promote rug hooking as an art form. I believe that referring to these pieces as Art Rugs, or hooked construction, is an important means of elevating the status of this art style and bringing it from the floor to the wall. Art Rugs: The "Art" of Playing Cards combines the rich tradition of rug hooking with the universal appeal of playing cards.

This international, invitational exhibit features the works of fifty-seven textile artists, with two of the pieces being collaborations. Each artist was committed to designing a 28" x 18" rug depicting one card from a deck of playing cards. This includes the thirteen cards from each suit (heart, clubs, diamonds, and spades), two jokers, and the back cover of the deck, for a total of fifty-five pieces. The rugs in this exhibit exemplify a wide variety of styles. They range from inventive to personal, nostalgic, feminist, and simply humorous. The artists were free to design their cards however they chose and the pieces were often autobiographical.

Four smaller suit symbols rugs were also created for the exhibit. Rug hooking kits of the heart suit symbol were made by Girl Scout Troop 522 of Flemington, New Jersey, to promote the art of rug hooking, with all proceeds from the sale of these kits going to the Girl Scouts of America.

This exhibit will travel from 2004-2008.
Photography by Linda Rae Coughlin.

8 of Hearts. By Rita Barnard, Ann Arbor, Michigan. Bleeding heart flower with its eight bleeding hearts.

10 of Diamonds. By Norma Batastini, Glen Ridge, New Jersey. Echoes of shapes and geometric patterns, created entirely from recycled materials.

King of Spades. By Patsy Becker, South Orleans, Massachusetts. A young "boy" King.

King of Diamonds. By Marilyn Bottjer, Eastchester, New York. "The House That Ruth Built," Yankee Stadium.

King of Clubs. By Elizabeth Black, Bentonville, Virginia. The true King of Beasts.

3 of Clubs. By Cilla Cameron, Nottingham, England. "Fan Club," developed into a hidden face.

8 of Clubs. By Claudia Casebolt, Lawrenceville, New Jersey. A family tree.

Ace of Diamonds. By Linda Rae Coughlin, Warren, New Jersey. Keeping with my woman series, "A Diamond Girl."

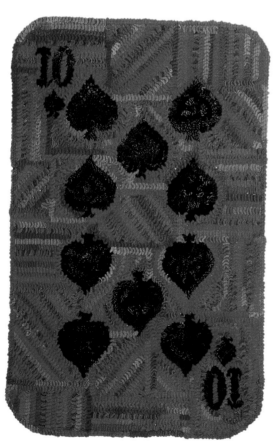

10 of Spades. By Cecilia Evan Clement, Manhattan, Kansas. Inspired by a Kaffe Fassett design.

4 of Hearts. By Kim Dubay, No. Yarmouth, Maine. "To create is to give my heart wings."

Ace of Hearts. By Gail Dufresne, Lambertville, New Jersey. All the things Gail loves to hook incorporated into one piece.

5 of Clubs. By Doris Eaton, Italy Cross, Nova Scotia, Canada. Influenced by the design symmetry in the Nova Scotia coast.

5 of Spades. By Susan Feller, Augusta, West Virginia. Inspired by the German's Fraktur designs—a pomegranate.

10 of Hearts. By Jeanne Field, Aurora, Ontario, Canada. Inspired by a pottery watering can given to Jeanne by her son.

4 of Spades. By Carol Feeney and Patti Ann Finch, Medford, New Jersey. A mother and daughter collaboration rug, with a garden theme.

Jack of Spades. By Deanne Fitzpatrick, Amherst, Nova Scotia, Canada. Inspired by Deanne's father who was a rebel and a gambler.

Keep your toolbox full. Take classes, attend lectures, read books, then do your art.

130

3 of Hearts. By Fumiyo Hachisuka, Tokyo, Japan. Love and peace, not the eternal triangle, was the inspiration for this design.

10 of Clubs. By Ann Hallett, Coldwater, Ontario, Canada. The beaver and the sugar leaf are distinctive Canadian icons.

Jack of Hearts. By Jane Halliwell, Portland, Maine. A turn-of-the-century fellow with his love.

Queen of Spades. By Rae Reynolds Harrell, Hinesburg, Vermont. A goddess with paranormal powers.

Queen of Hearts. By Nancy L. Himmelsbach, Hampton Bays, New York. A queen of many faces.

Ace of Clubs. By Linda Pietz and Nola Heidbreder, St. Louis, Missouri. Two sisters collaborated in the symbolic piece honoring the "Gateway to the West."

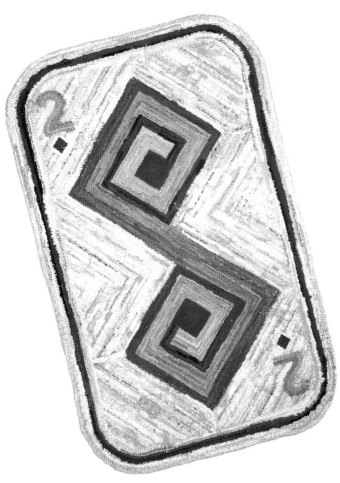

2 of Diamonds. By Peg Irish, Waquoit, Massachusetts. "Snake Eyes" incorporates over one hundred different materials.

2 of Clubs. By Carrie Bell Jacobus, Oradell, New Jersey. Freedom and possibilities are the goal of "Two Wish Upon A Club."

Ace of Spades. By Tracy Jamar, New York City, New York. A memorial to a horse named "Arrow."

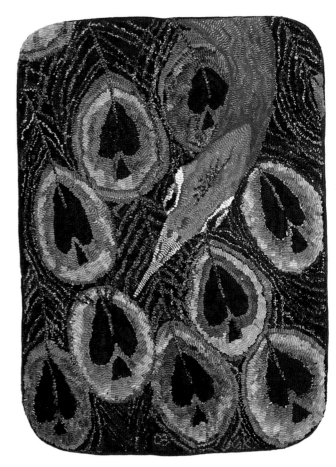

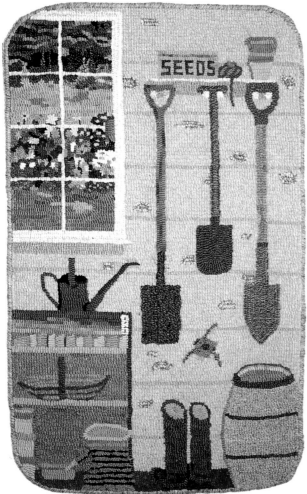

9 of Spades. By Wanda Kerr, Wiarton, Ontario, Canada. A "dark" card of the Tarot Cards, this symbolizes immortality, confidence, and beauty.

3 of Spades. By Diane S. Kelly, Dorset, Vermont. A view from the potting shed.

9 of Clubs. By Stephanie Ashworth Krauss, Montpelier, Vermont. A love of Victorian designs and pansies evolved into a garden of pansies.

8 of Spades. By Maryanne Lincoln, Wrentham, Massachusetts. Clock hands and leaf designs gathered from the yard inspired this piece.

6 of Spades. By Lea H. McCrone, Malvern, Pennsylvania. "For Quinn, our yellow lab, after she had her six puppies and then was spayed."

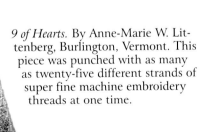

9 of Hearts. By Anne-Marie W. Littenberg, Burlington, Vermont. This piece was punched with as many as twenty-five different strands of super fine machine embroidery threads at one time.

Jack of Clubs. By Michele Micarelli, New Haven, Connecticut. This out-of-the-closet Jack is now known as Jackie.

3 of Diamonds. By Pat Merikallio, Capitola, California. A love of color and a little cat inspired this rug.

Queen of Spades. By Jo-Ann Millen, Boxford, Massachusetts. Inspired by fond memories of searching for lucky four-leaf clovers with her dad.

2 of Hearts. By Polly Minick, Naples, Florida. A simple design in patriotic colors.

7 of Clubs. By Kim Nixon, Maryville, Tennessee. A "club" tree with its seven crows, feeding on the scattered seeds of another harvest.

7 of Spades. By Amy Oxford, Cornwall, Vermont. Yes, a leopard can change its spots...to spades.

7 of Diamonds. By Deanie Pass, Minneapolis, Minnesota. "7 Years Alas Since Breast Cancer."

5 of Hearts. By Diane Phillips, Fairport, New York. "A radiance that comes from having five times the generosity of one heart."

4 of Clubs. By Nancy Reding, Montgomery Village, Maryland. "The Adirondack Fishing Club," with its four cub family members.

4 of Diamonds. By Denise Reithofer, Burlington, Ontario, Canada. Inspired by an interest in divination and the book *History of Cards*, by Catherine Perry Hargrave.

2 of Spades. By Emily K. Robertson, Falmouth, Massachusetts. Emily in her garden with her two garden spades.

8 of Diamonds. By Heather Ritchie, Richmond North York, England. "A Diamond is a Girl's Best Friend."

5 of Diamonds. By Olga Rothschild, Duxbury, Massachusetts. Inspired by an Oaxaca design.

Jack of Diamonds. By Miriam "Dolly" Rowe, Alexandria, Virginia. Inspired by Norman Laliberte's vivid colors.

6 of Diamonds. By Alice Rudell, New York City, New York. A repeat of the design elements of the diamond and the number six.

Queen of Diamonds. By Eric H. Sandberg, Gainesville, Florida. A tribute to Elizabeth Taylor.

Joker. By Jule Marie Smith, Ballston Spa, New York. The Red Joker, juggling his J's.

7 of Hearts. By Susan L. Smidt, Salem, Massachusetts. The faces of seven of Susan's good friends.

9 of Diamonds. By Abby Vakay, Alexandria, Virginia. Nine punched abstract diamonds form sailboats on the sea.

6 of Hearts. By Sharon L. Townsend, Altoona, Iowa. "Hand and Foot at Freddy's," dedicated to Sharon's 90+ mother and her five card playing friends.

6 of Clubs. By Margo White, Indianapolis, Indiana. Cats and birds are favorite themes in Margo's art.

Joker. 28" x 18". By Ann Winterling, Concord, New Hampshire. The Black Joker, a Renaissance jester.

King of Hearts. By Patty Yoder, Tinmouth, Vermont. One last sheep, the strong and powerful King of Hearts.

Back of Deck. By Rose Wirtz, Rockaway, New Jersey. "Flip Side," a unique natural dyed hit or miss piece.

Heart. 14" x 9". By Lisa Mims, Flemington, New Jersey. Suit Symbol.

Diamond. 14" x 9". By Lisa Mims, Flemington, New Jersey. Suit Symbol.

Club. 14" x 9". By Lisa Mims, Flemington, New Jersey. Suit Symbol.

Spade. 14" x 9". By Lisa Mims, Flemington, New Jersey. Suit Symbol.

Chapter Nine

Sign Rugs

Sign Rugs by Karl and Mary Jo Gimber

Karl and Mary Jo Gimber of Carversville, Pennsylvania, have had a long standing interest in decorative American arts of the eighteenth and nineteenth centuries. This series represents old tavern, farm, and trade signs. Historic flags, gravestone rubbings, old weathervanes, and folk art are also sources of inspiration for many of this couple's rugs. Their rugs are almost exclusively made with "as is" recycled wool in keeping with their love of the old.

Photography by Linda Rae Coughlin.

Don't Tread On Me. 22" x 28". By Karl and Mary Jo Gimber, Carversville, Pennsylvania. 2003. The rattlesnake was a favorite symbol with American colonists and its origin as an American emblem is a curious feature of our natural history. This rug reflects one of the variations of the flag of the Continental Navy.

Old Homestead. 23" x 28". By Karl and Mary Jo Gimber, Carversville, Pennsylvania. 2004. "This design emerged from a series of sketches drawn on the back of a placemat at our favorite restaurant."

Temperance. 19" x 32". By Karl and Mary Jo Gimber, Carversville, Pennsylvania. 2003. Adapted from a tavern sign of the Temperance Hotel. When the Temperance Movement began in the 1840s, supporters stopped serving distilled beverages, but they often continued to serve wine, beer, and cider. Temperance tavern signs frequently contained patriotic images.

Liberty Tavern. 25" x 32". By Karl and Mary Jo Gimber, Carversville, Pennsylvania. 2004. During the Constitutional Convention in 1787, the President of the convention sat on a chair with a sunburst on the crest. Ben Franklin was said to have commented that during the debate he was unsure if the sun was rising or setting. At the successful conclusion of the debate, he said that the sun was certainly rising.

Bulle Tavern. 24" x 30". By Karl and Mary Jo Gimber, Carversville, Pennsylvania. 2004. Inspired by an old weathervane and nineteenth century English paintings of prize bulls. The original Bulle Tavern was located in colonial Philadelphia.

Crofut's Inn. 32" x 34". By Karl and Mary Jo Gimber, Carversville, Pennsylvania. 2004. The image in this rug is a rebus. Combining the crow, the foot, and the inn gives you Crow foot's Inn or Crofut's Inn. Inspired by the actual Crofut's Inn sign in the collection of the Connecticut Historical Society.

Blue Hill Hotel. 28" x 31". By Karl and Mary Jo Gimber, Carversville, Pennsylvania. 2004. The Blue Hill Hotel was located in Blue Hill, Maine. The image was adapted from an 1825 painting entitled "The Plantation" in the collection of the Metropolitan Museum.

Goat in Boots Inn. 27" x 32". By Karl and Mary Jo Gimber, Carversville, Pennsylvania. 2004. The original British tavern sign is attributed to artist George Morland. The goat was inspired by a nineteenth century weathervane, with boots added by Mary Jo.

Free Kittens. 23" x 48". By Karl and Mary Jo Gimber, Carversville, Pennsylvania. 2005. Adapted from a farm sign. This "hit or miss" background was a way to use the surplus cut wool strips from other rug projects.

Silent Woman Tavern. 28" x 24". By Karl and Mary Jo Gimber, Carversville, Pennsylvania. 2005. The Silent Woman and The Good Woman were popular names of eighteenth and nineteenth century taverns, all bearing the images of headless women.

> *Inspiration is everywhere, if we just take the time to look for it.*

Pigs 4 Sale. 23" x 28". By Karl and Mary Jo Gimber, Carversville, Pennsylvania. 2005. Adapted from an old farm sign, these colorful images can be seen on many country roads.

Here Lyes Ye Body. 23" x 28". By Karl and Mary Jo Gimber, Carversville, Pennsylvania. 2005. Inspired by early New England gravestone rubbings.

Boots and Shoes. 27" x 33". By Karl and Mary Jo Gimber, Carversville, Pennsylvania. 2005. Adapted from a nineteenth century cobbler's sign from upstate New York. This rug has personal significance to Karl, as his parents owned a shoe store and shoe repair business.

Red Cock Tavern. 24" x 26". By Karl and Mary Jo Gimber, Carversville, Pennsylvania. 2005. Inspired by old wooden weathervanes from New England.

Seven Stars Inn. 23" x 28". By Karl and Mary Jo Gimber, Carversville, Pennsylvania. 2005. Inns with "Star" in their names were popular in old England and Revolutionary America.

Blue Anchor Tavern. 33" x 23". By Karl and Mary Jo Gimber, Carversville, Pennsylvania. 2005. The Blue Anchor Tavern was one of the first taverns built in Philadelphia and was under construction when William Penn visited in 1682. Inspired by an eighteenth century tavern sign in the collection of the Connecticut Historical Society.

Chapter Ten

Of Universal Appeal

Mandalas and Sacred Geometry by Charlene Marsh

Both a fiber artist and a painter, Charlene Marsh has been a full time artist since 1987 and has been featured in films and documentaries. Her commissioned work can be found in both private collections and public institutions and has even been shown at the White House in Washington, D.C.

About four years ago, she started a new series of fiber pieces focusing on the chakras, sacred geometry, and mandalas, which she writes about here:

The mandala is a Sanskrit term meaning "sacred circle" and represents the womb of creation. The mandala is divided by lines and circles to form multiple layers of patterns that connect us with the inherent order of the universe despite the seeming chaos and diversity.

Sacred geometry involves the five platonics, plus the sphere, from which all life comes into form. Equilateral sides define each platonic and at the root of every form in our reality is a platonic geometric shape. The use of sacred geometry helps us tap into the infinite order of the universe on a subconscious level.

A visual symphony results from the use of the mandala and geometry that serves as an interdimensional gateway to higher realms and elevated ways of thinking. Combining the mandala and sacred geometry connects us with universal wisdom and knowledge.

This series is tufted with hand-dyed wool and metallic yarns.

Photography and artist statement courtesy of Charlene Marsh.

Aum Shanti. 45" x 81". By Charlene Marsh, Nashville, Indiana. 2003.

Om Jai Ma Gaia. 44" x 44". By Charlene Marsh, Nashville, Indiana. 2004.

Shakti Yantra. 44" x 45". By Charlene Marsh, Nashville, Indiana. 2004.

Jai Ram. 45" x 46". By Charlene Marsh, Nashville, Indiana. 2004.

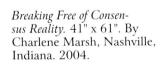

Breaking Free of Consensus Reality. 41" x 61". By Charlene Marsh, Nashville, Indiana. 2004.

Shifting Frequencies. 32" x 46". By Charlene Marsh, Nashville, Indiana. 2004.

Om Tara #2. 22" x 44". By Charlene Marsh, Nashville, Indiana. 2005.

Time Fold. 24" x 36". By Charlene Marsh, Nashville, Indiana. 2005.

Acadian Legends - Children's Rugs

In 2004, about 150 children from two Canadian schools were initiated into the art of rug hooking by members of "Les Hookeuses du Bor'de'lo," a group of Acadian women artists from New Brunswick, Canada. Each student completed a small design of a house and their pieces were part of a large exhibit called "Rugs Have Their Stories" (see next section). Featured here are six examples from the two schools. Each piece is 12" x 12" and was hooked with wool, t-shirts, and yarn into a linen foundation. Artists remained anonymous.

Photography by Christian Ouellet.

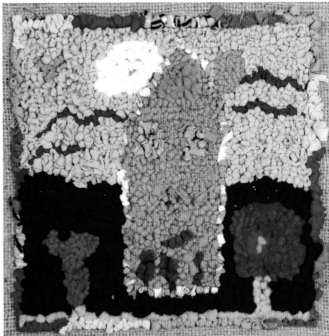

By St. Thérèsa School, Dieppe, New Brunswick, Canada. Anonymous, Grade 3.

By St. Thérèsa School, Dieppe, New Brunswick, Canada. Anonymous, Grade 3.

By St. Thérèsa School, Dieppe, New Brunswick, Canada. Anonymous, Grade 3.

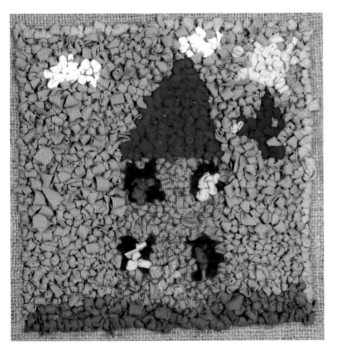

By Père-Edgar-T.-Leblanc School, Grand-Barachois, New Brunswick, Canada. Anonymous, Grade 5.

Acadian Legends – Rugs Have Their Stories

"Laisson parler les tapis – Rugs Have Their Stories" is the title for this series. In 2004, the Acadian people celebrated the 400th anniversary of Acadie, an area that includes portions of Canada's east coast. To mark this celebration, the rug hooking group called "Les Hookeuses du Bor'de'lo" was looking for a special group fiber project. The project they chose consisted of working with grade school children (ages eight to eleven) in two schools. The children first listened to an Acadian short story or legend, then drew or painted a picture under the guidance of an art teacher. "Les Hookeuses du Bor'de'lo" subsequently used these drawings for their hooking project. The results were amazing. Featured here are sixteen of the forty-six tapestries illustrating a variety of Acadian legends and stories.

Photography by Christian Ouellet.

Phantom Boat. 17" x 15". By Thérèsa Arsenault Léger, Shediac, New Brunswick, Canada. 2004. "Everything was calm one beautiful morning in 1820. In the distance, a boat appeared in the Bay of Chaleurs. As the waves increased in size, the boat slowly broke apart, and turned into a ball of fire. Traveling at full speed towards the coast, it stopped short some one hundred feet from the coast and suddenly disappeared without a trace." An Acadian legend, adapted from a watercolor by Alexis Léger, Grade 6.

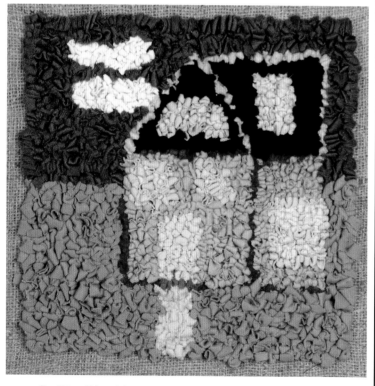

By Père-Edgar-T.-Leblanc School, Grand-Barachois, New Brunswick, Canada. Anonymous, Grade 5.

By Père-Edgar-T.-Leblanc School, Grand-Barachois, New Brunswick, Canada. Anonymous, Grade 6.

The Legend of the Petitcodiac River. 15" x 17". By Line Godbout, Shediac, New Brunswick, Canada. 2004. "The King Lobster gave thanks to the Creator. But the Creator declared: 'The river which you have conquered will no longer produce fish and will remain muddy to remind you of the war. Furthermore, you will never be able to live in it. Finally, as a symbol of your cruelty, you will turn red upon death, the color of the blood you have shed.'" A native legend, adapted from a watercolor by Jordan Duguay, Grade 6.

Phantom Boat. 17" x 15". By Éveline Haché-Lachance, Cocague, New Brunswick, Canada. 2004. An Acadian legend, adapted from a watercolor by Erika Hickey, Grade 6.

Ti-Jean. 15" x 17". By Évangéline Savoie, Grand Barachois, New Brunswick, Canada. 2004. In the Acadian popular tradition, Ti-Jean is always the same little fellow, sometimes strong, sometimes sly, sometimes having supernatural powers to overcome obstacles in his way. An Acadian legend, adapted from a watercolor by Josée Roy, Grade 6.

The Legend of the Petitcodiac River. 15" x 17". By Line Godbout, Shediac, New Brunswick, Canada. 2004. "A long time ago, a huge eel lived in the Petitcodiac River. Her body had sculpted its banks, creating long curves. During this same period, a giant lobster lived in the bay of Fundy. He was considered the King of the Ocean. The Lobster King decided to conquer this river and a ferocious battle followed with the eel. The river turned muddy and the Queen Eel started to tire. One day, the King won." A native legend, adapted from a watercolor by Alexis Léger, Grade 6.

The Flying Clothesline. 15" x 17". By Nicole Butler, Moncton, New Brunswick, Canada. 2004. "Blown away by the wind, Mariette and her clothesline find themselves at the crossroad of the East and West. Young Asghar, who has never seen such kites, takes Mariette to discover his city. Mariette's clothesline touches all the colors of the Orient. Upon her return, Mariette's clothesline brushes the village houses, the church, and the general store, unloading along the way all the clothes she picked up in the city she visited. By doing so, all the buildings in her town turned the colors of the rainbow. Since then, the Acadians have never been short of colors for their houses." An Acadian story by Myriame Le Yamani, adapted from a watercolor by Julie McIntyre, Grade 5.

The Great Deportation. 15" x 17". By Florine Gagnon, Irishtown, New Brunswick, Canada. 2004. "In 1755, more than 7000 French settlers living in Acadia, who refused to swear allegiance to the British crown, were herded into boats and sent into the hinterland. After the deportation, some settled in Québec and in France, while others made it as far as Georgia and Louisiana." An adaptation of a Henry Longfellow poem, adapted from a watercolor by Marie-Josée Léger, Grade 6.

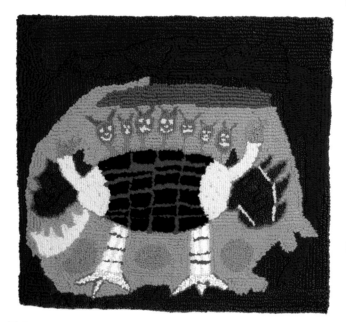

Ti-Jean. 15" x 17". By Pierrette Bortolussi, Moncton, New Brunswick, Canada. 2004. "Ti-Jean did not listen to the princess's objections and sat down near the cliff to wait for the arrival of the beast. After an hour, he saw her coming. She was huge and was wearing proudly her seven heads which formed a half circle around her body like the majestic tail of the peacock…" An Acadian legend, adapted from a watercolor by Randy-Goguen Léger, Grade 6.

The Great Deportation. 15" x 17". By Nicole Butler, Moncton, New Brunswick, Canada. 2004. "Heartbroken by the deportation, young Évangéline Bellefontaine searches in vain across North America for her beloved Gabriel Lajeunesse. To ease her pain, she becomes a nun and takes care of the sick. After many years, she finally is reunited with her lover on his deathbed." An adaptation of a Henry Longfellow poem, adapted from a watercolor by Adèle Cormier, Grade 6.

The Grand-Pré Rug. 15" x 17". By Grace Ward, Grande-Digue, New Brunswick, Canada. 2004. If you ever go to Grand-Pré on Christmas eve, look for the little chapel. An Acadian story by Réjean Aucoin and Jean-Claude Tremblay, adapted from a watercolor by Émilie Cyr, Grade 3.

The Grand-Pré Rug. 17" x 15". By Jeanne Bourgeois, Grande-Digue, New Brunswick, Canada. 2004. "On Christmas eve, two young children take off in the nocturnal sky trying to recover the twelve strands of wool needed to complete the rug of Grand-Pré. Flying amongst the stars in the magic bag of Johnny, the magical postman, they visit the four corners of Acadia. Each stop brings them closer to the conclusion of their search and to their ancestors as well." An Acadian story by Réjean Aucoin and Jean-Claude Tremblay, adapted from a watercolor by Kayla Jubinville, Ggrade 3.

The Grand-Pré Rug. 15" x 17". By Danielle Ouellet, Grande-Digue, New Brunswick, Canada. 2004. "On Christmas eve, if you see lights or hear violins, guitars or mandolins, you will know that the ancestors are back celebrating Christmas…now the children have hooked the last strands of yarn on the Grand-Pré rug." An Acadian story by Réjean Aucoin and Jean-Claude Tremblay, adapted from a watercolor by Janelle Cormier, Grade 3.

The Grand-Pré Rug. 17" x 15". By Marielle R. Poirier, Grande-Digue, New Brunswick, Canada. 2004. The Acadians of Grand-Pré deported in 1755. An Acadian story by Réjean Aucoin and Jean-Claude Tremblay, adapted from a water-color by Dominique Rioux, Grade 3.

L'Arbre est dans ses feuilles. 15" x 17". By Danielle Ouellet, Grande-Digue, New Brunswick, Canada. 2004. Beautiful song by Acadian Cajun songwriter and interpreter Zachary Richard about love in our hearts and what we can discover in a tree. An Acadian song by Zachary Richard, adapted from a watercolor by Chantal Saulnier, Grade 3.

L'Arbre est dans ses feuilles. 15" x 17". By Florine Gagnon, Irishtown, New Brunswick, Canada. 2004. An Acadian song by Zachary Richard, adapted from a watercolor by Cynthia Martin, Grade 3.

L'Arbre est dans ses feuilles. 15" x 17". By Danielle Ouellet, Grande-Digue, New Brunswick, Canada. 2004. An Acadian song by Zachary Richard, adapted from a watercolor by Jérémie Brun, Grade 6.

Index of Artists